JN125958

NHK NEWSLINE 4

Tatsuroh Yamazaki
Stella M. Yamazaki

KINSEIDO

Kinseido Publishing Co., Ltd.
3-21 Kanda Jimbo-cho, Chiyoda-ku,
Tokyo 101-0051, Japan

First published 2021 by Kinseido Publishing Co., Ltd.

Video materials NHK (Japan Broadcasting Corporation)

Images
Muse Village (p. 33, middle), Shimane Art Museum (p. 81, top: *Sagawa Kikunojō III as Oren, the daughter of Masamune*, middle: *Perspective Picture of the Play of the Founder of Kabuki in the Eastern Capital*), Shochiku Co., Ltd. (p. 85, p. 87)

Authors and publisher are grateful to NHK Global Media Services, Inc. and all the interviewees who appeared on the news.

はじめに

NHK NEWSLINE のテキストシリーズが刊行されてから、今回で４冊目を迎えることができた。皆様のご支援に心より感謝申し上げる。

新型コロナウイルス（COVID-19）感染拡大による未曽有のパンデミックが、世界中の経済活動や社会の仕組み・運営に激変を来している。大学なども授業のオンライン化が急速に進み、新たな時代の局面に向き合わざるをえなくなった。

こうした中でも、グローバルなコミュニケーション手段として確固たる地位を築いた英語の重要性は日々増すばかりである。今では英語などの学習者の習得状況を測るCEFR（セファール「ヨーロッパ言語共通参照枠」）という国際標準規格も普及してきている。

外出自粛が増える中、今は在宅してじっくり実力を養う好機ととらえることができる。オンラインの英会話レッスンは、安全にしてかつ効果が期待できる。それと並行して、会話の前提となるリスニング能力を伸ばす本書のような教材も利用できる。

アウトプット技能は、実際はインプット技能とは別物ではなく表裏一体の関係にある。会話で言うならば、「話す」技能はその基礎に「聞く」技能が前提とされるということである。どんな表現が通じるしぜんな英語なのかを聞き取り、（文字を通すなどして）それを覚えれば、すぐに自分の英語の表現の一部として発話できるのである。そういう意味でこれからますます、英語リスニングの重要性が強調されていくことになるであろう。

会話は音声のインプットとアウトプットの合わせ技だが、外国語は徹底的に聞いて模倣するという姿勢が常に必要である。従って伝統的な反復練習や文型練習は、語学学習者にとって必修である。目で追うだけではなく何回か反復して「音読」しておこう。音読しておけば記憶に定着しやすく、会話でもとっさの時に出てくるという利点がある。学習者にとって外国語の会話は（運動競技と同様に）スキルであり、練習によって積み上げた「記憶」が頼りなのである。

本書はリスニングを中心課題に据えたニュースの視聴覚教材である。ニュースはNHK海外向け放送のNEWSLINEから採択し、適切な長さに編集した。この番組は現代日本の主な出来事や経済、文化、科学の最近の動向などを簡潔にまとめており好評を博している。

語学は授業中の学習だけではじゅうぶんではない。本書のニュース映像はオンラインで視聴可能なので、自宅で納得するまで繰り返し見てほしい。その際、まず完成したスクリプト（News Storyの穴埋め問題終了後）を見ながら音声と意味の対応を頭に入れ、その後は文字を見ないで聞くという作業が必要である。この繰り返しが何回かあれば、文字なしで映像音声の理解ができるという快感が味わえるようになる。

末筆ながら、本書の作成に関して金星堂編集部をはじめ関係スタッフの方々に大変お世話になった。さらに出版にあたってNHK、株式会社NHKグローバルメディアサービスの皆様にも映像提供などでご協力をいただいた。ここに厚くお礼を申し上げる。

2021年１月　　　　　編著者　山﨑達朗／ Stella M. Yamazaki

本書の構成とねらい

本書は全部で15単元（units）からなり、各単元とも、①日本語のイントロダクション、② Words & Phrases、③ Before You Watch、④ Watch the News、⑤ Understand the News、⑥ News Story、⑦ Review the Key Expressions、⑧ Discussion Questions という構成になっている。このうち①と②は説明で、③〜⑧が練習問題である。

① 日本語のイントロダクション

この短い日本語の説明（140語前後）は、ニュースの要点を把握することを目的としている。外国語のリスニングには、何がどのように飛び出してくるかわからないという緊張と不安が常に伴うので、このように限られた背景知識（background knowledge）でも、予め準備があると安心感が出るものである。

② Words & Phrases

比較的難しいか、カギになる語彙や熟語などを学習する。ここで意味的、文法的知識をつけておけば、ニュースを聞いた場合に戸惑いは少なくなる。必要に応じて簡単な例文も入れてある。

③ Before You Watch

ニュース映像を見る前に、その予備知識を獲得したり話題を膨らませたりする意味で単元ごとに違った課題が用意してある。内容としては、日常会話表現の学習であったり、社会・文化に特有な語彙を英語でどう言うかといった課題であったりする。方法としても活動に興味が持てるように、ややゲーム的な要素も入れるようにしてある。英語の語彙を縦横に並んだアルファベット表から見つけ出すタスクや、クロスワードの活用もその例である。

④ Watch the News — First Viewing

ここで初めてクラスで映像を見るわけだが、課題はニュース内容の大きな流れや要点の理解が主となる基本的把握である。設問が３つあり、各問とも内容に合っていればT（= True）、合っていなければF（= False）を選択し、問題文の真偽を判断する。外国語のリスニングはしぜんに耳から入ってくるということがないので、集中して聞く必要がある。必要に応じて随時、視聴の回数を増やしたり、問題と関連する箇所を教師が集中的に見せたりするということが過去の経験から有効である。

⑤ Understand the News — Second Viewing

同じニュース映像をもう一度見るが、内容についてのやや詳細な質問となっている。次の２種類の下位区分がある。ここも必要に応じ、複数回のリスニングを考慮してほしい。

1 最初の視聴と比べて今度は選択肢が３つになっており、内容もより詳細にわたる設問が用意してある。各問、右端の３枚の写真は、参考にはなるが、問題を解く上でリスニングのキーとなる部分の映像とは限らないので注意してほしい。

2 単元によって、何種類か様々な形式の設問が用意してある。いずれもニュース内容や単語の用法の確認を目的としている。例えばニュースのまとめとなる「概要」や「入手情報の順序づけ」、要点となる数字の記入などである。さらに、設問によっては、ややゲーム的な要素を考慮し、アルファベットの並べ替え (unscrambling) を入れている。

⑥ News Story

これはニュース映像に対応するスクリプトであるが、完全なものにするには「穴埋め問題」を解く必要がある。問題は合計７問で、各問題に６箇所位の空所がある。解答するには、スタジオでややゆっくり読まれた音声 CD をクラスで（各２回繰り返し）聞きながら書き取り作業（dictation）をする。スクリプトのそれぞれの問題には、右端におおまかな日本語訳（数字以外）がつけてあるのでヒントになる。書き取りが完成すればニュース映像の全文が目で確かめられるが、スクリプトは映像を見る前に読むことはせず、まず何回か視聴して上記④と⑤の設問に解答した後に、この穴埋めに挑戦してほしい。

⑦ Review the Key Expressions

ここでは、映像で出てきた単語や熟語などのうち応用性のある表現に習熟することがねらいである。そのような重要表現の意味や用法を確実にするとともに、英作文があまり負担なく身につくように単語を与える「整序問題」形式（４問）を採用した。ただし選択肢の中に錯乱肢（distractors）を１語入れ、適度に難しくしてある。文例は当該単元の話題とは関係なく、いろいろな場面の設定になっている。

⑧ Discussion Questions

最後の問題として、クラス内での話し合いに使える話題を２つ用意してある。当該単元に関連した身近な話題が提示してあるので、短く簡単な英語で自分の考えを表現してみる、というのがねらいである。（ご指導の先生へ：クラスによっては宿題として、話すことを次回までに考えておくというスタンスでもよいと思われる。この話し合いの課題は、人数や時間などクラス設定との兼ね合いから、用途に応じて柔軟に扱うのがよいと考えられる。）

NHK NEWSLINE 4

Contents

UNIT 1 Making Waves with a Magical Instrument

不屈のテルミン奏者

ロシアの電子楽器テルミンの同時演奏者数でギネス世界記録が更新された。テルミン奏者竹内正実さんが中心になり多くの愛好家に参加を募り、ベートーベンの「第九」が演奏されたのだ。使用されたのは小型の「マトリョミン」という楽器で、竹内さんがテルミンの機能を民芸品のマトリョーシカに組み込む形で開発した。

● Words & Phrases

CD 02

- ☐ **deftly**　巧みに、器用に
- ☐ to **flutter**　～を振る、ひらひらさせる
- ☐ **antennae**　アンテナ、触覚〈この意味での複数形〉
- ☐ to **catch up with**　～に追いつく
- ☐ **esoteric**　秘伝的な、奥が深い
- ☐ to **merge with**　（～と）結合する、合体する
- ☐ **ethereal**　霊妙な、この世のものとは思えない
- ☐ to **set off**　出発する、出かける
  He *set off* for home after so many years of study abroad.
  彼は長年の海外留学の後で帰途についた。
- ☐ to **incorporate**　～を組み込む
  Daiki *incorporated* his suggestions into the report.
  大輝は自分の提案をその報告書に組み入れた。
- ☐ to **take off**　《口語》スタートする
- ☐ **setback**　つまづき，後退
- ☐ **paralyzed**　麻痺した　　☐ to **reaffirm**　～(の価値）を再確認する

Before You Watch

以下は、音楽や音に関する語彙が含まれる表現です。下の枠内から適切な単語を選び、空所に入れましょう。なお、余分な単語もあります。

1. 君のお父さんは、君が彼のお金をテレビ［ビデオ］ゲームのため浪費したことを知った。君は、自分が招いた結果を受け入れるべきだ。
Your father found out you wasted his money on video games. You had better be ready to face the ( ).

2. 彼の顔は覚えていないが、名前を聞いたらピンと来た。
I don't remember his face, but his name rings a ( ).

3. 内部告発者によって、その会社の悪事があばかれた。
The company's wrongdoings were exposed by a ( ).

4. ステイシーは私が学部長と強いコネがあると知って、すぐに態度を変えた。
Stacy changed her ( ) as soon as she learned that I had a lot of pull with the dean.

5. 会社の私の上司はよく自慢話をする［ほらを吹く］。
My boss at the company often blows his own ( ).

6. 感動的なスピーチをありがとうございます。言葉が心に響きました。
Thank you for your moving speech. Your words really struck a ( ).

bell	chord	horn	music	piano
player	tune	whistleblower		

Watch the News

First Viewing

ニュースを見て、内容と合っているものはT、違っているものはFを選びましょう。

1. The theremin is an electronic musical instrument created a century ago. [T / F]
2. A musical instrument was incorporated into traditional Japanese dolls. [T / F]
3. Takeuchi has trained at least 800 people how to play the theremin. [T / F]

Understand the News　Second Viewing

1 ニュースをもう一度見て、各問の空所に入る適切な選択肢を a ～ c から選びましょう。

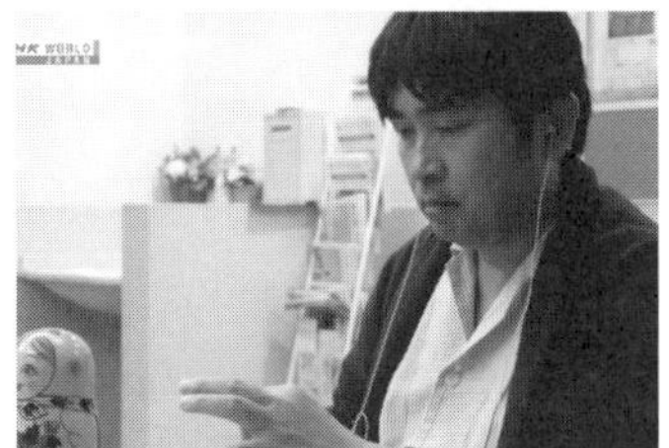

1. Leon Theremin was a ____.

a. Russian medical doctor
b. Russian scholar in physics
c. music teacher at a Russian college

2. Takeuchi went to Russia to ____.

a. study more about the theremin
b. manufacture matryomin in 2000
c. set a world record for theremin playing

3. In 2016, Takeuchi ____.

a. became seriously ill in Russia
b. had a financial problem
c. became physically disabled

2 以下はニュースの概要です。空所に適切な単語を書き入れましょう。語頭の文字は与えてあります。

The theremin is a Russian (**e** 1) musical instrument named after its inventor. When you play it, you don't touch the instrument, but hold your fingers (**m** 2). Masami Takeuchi is a famous player of the instrument and learned to play the music from a relative of Theremin. He also incorporated the instrument into cute (**m** 3) dolls to attract more people. Although he unfortunately suffered a (**s** 4), he continued his involvement with theremin music as a (**p** 5). He saw his dream come true when his followers, close to 300, set a (**w** 6) record by playing theremin music all together.

3 CD の音声を聞いて、次ページ News Story の❶～❼の文中にある空所に適切な単語を書き入れましょう。音声は２回繰り返されます。　CD 03

● News Story

Anchor: Next, we'll be talking about an unusual instrument, the theremin, the world's first electronic musical instrument. ❶ Developed 100 years ago by Russian physicist Leon Theremin, (　　　[1]) (　　　[2]) (　　　[3]) (　　　[4]). Instead, players **deftly flutter** their fingertips midair between a pair of **antennae**. We **caught up with** the man who made Japan the land of this **esoteric** instrument.

> ❶ 接触する必要がない

Narrator: While the theremin has been around since the 1920s, in Japan it later **merged with** Russian matryoshka dolls, finding new enthusiasts, around 6,000 today.

❷ In September about 300 of them (　　　[1]) (　　　[2]) (　　　[3]) (　　　[4]) (　　　[5]) (　　　[6]). The challenge was set by Masami Takeuchi, an expert and professional player who introduced the instrument to Japan over 20 years ago.

> ❷ 世界記録を破るため集まった

***Masami Takeuchi* (*Professional theremin player*):** No matter how much imagination I could have summoned, I could never have imagined a future with something like this and so many people.

Narrator: Pursuing the **ethereal** sound, Takeuchi **set off** for Russia in 1993 to study under Theremin's relative.

Takeuchi: The sound of a theremin is like water or a gel. It's a sound without a shape. You make music by adding order and making the shape beautiful. I don't think there's any other instrument like that.

Narrator: ❸ When Takeuchi returned to Japan in the 90s, (　　　[1]) (　　　[2]) (　　　[3]) (　　　[4]) (　　　[5]) (　　　[6]). To win fans, he **incorporated** the theremin in the shape of charming matryoshka dolls and launched the first generation of

> ❸ 彼は楽器を広めようと決断した

his matryomin in the year 2000.

❹ It was a hit, especially among women ([1]) ([2]) ([3]) ([4]) ([5]), and theremin playing **took off**. He has trained some 800 people since.

❹ 電子音楽に夢中になった

In 2016 Takeuchi faced a major **setback**. Mid-performance he suffered a stroke. ❺ With his right side **paralyzed**, he ([1]) ([2]) ([3]) ([4]) ([5]), but his students from across Japan rallied around him.

❺ 演奏者としての彼のキャリアは終わったと思った

Takeuchi: This wasn't the end for me. In fact, it **reaffirmed** my reason for living.

Narrator: ❻ Now he's on ([1]) ([2]) ([3]) ([4]) ([5]) ([6]), bringing together nearly 300 players in the hopes of creating a world record. Theremin's family flies in from Russia.

❻ プロデューサーとしての新しい役目［使命］

Natalia Theremin (Leon Theremin's daughter): I am so happy to collaborate with Masami. I'm looking forward to our performance.

Narrator: Beethoven's *Symphony Number 9: Ode to Joy.** ❼ Twenty-six years ago ([1]) ([2]) ([3]) ([4]) ([5]) ([6]) theremin ([7]) in Japan. Now there are hundreds. And the defining moment: the ensemble sets a world record.

❼（テルミンの）演奏者は一人しか知られていなかった

Takeuchi: I will never stop looking for beautiful sounds. We set a new record, but I won't stop here.

Note

＊ 交響曲第９番「歓喜の歌」

Review the Key Expressions

各問、選択肢から適切な単語を選び、英文を完成させましょう。なお、余分な単語が１語ずつあります。

1. ラインは役に立つコミュニケーションの形だと思われるかもしれないが［～の一方で］、欠点もある。

( ) LINE may ( ) to ( ) a useful ( ) of communication, it does have ( ) ( ).

drawbacks be seem form good its while

2. いくら忙しくても、今年のクラスの同窓会には出席するつもりだ。

I'll ( ) this year's class ( ), ( ) ( ) ( ) busy I ( ).

am no attend how reunion whatever matter

3. パンデミック［世界的伝染病］のせいで、全国（規模の）野球大会が中止になった。みんな１年間ずっと楽しみにしていたのに。

( ) ( ) the pandemic, the national baseball tournament was ( ). Everyone was ( ) ( ) to it the ( ) year.

to whole due forward cancelled looking after

4. 大学の新卒者が、自分たちの能力をより十分に生かせる仕事を探している。

New college ( ) are ( ) ( ) jobs ( ) they ( ) use their abilities ( ) fully.

where more looking when can graduates for

● Discussion Questions

1. What is your favorite kind of music: classical, rock, jazz or pop?

2. Are you good at group activities? If yes, what kind? If not, why not?

UNIT 2

Backstage Tour with Augmented Reality Stars

AR アイドルの裏側に迫る

ARP は拡張現実により誕生した４人組の AR ダンス＆ボーカルグループである。彼らは単なるアニメではなく、観客とのインタラクティブなトークができるファン参加型ライブを得意とする。このパフォーマンスを可能にするにはさまざまな分野のプロが関わっているが、今回はその舞台裏を紹介する。

● Words & Phrases

CD 04

- □ **augmented reality** (= AR)　拡張現実〈現実空間にデジタル情報を重ね合わせて表示する技術〉
- □ **interactive**　インタラクティブ、双方向の、対話式の
- □ **app**　アプリ
- □ **deal**　協約、約束事
- □ **motion sensor**　人感センサー〈赤外線や超音波などを使い、人の所在を検知するセンサー〉
- □ **voice actor**　声優
- □ to **matter**　重要［大切］である
  "Black Lives *Matter*" is an American movement against racial discrimination.
  「黒人の命は大切」は人種差別に対するアメリカの抗議運動である。
- □ to **synchronize**　シンクロする、同期する
- □ **gig**　《口語》演奏会
  Many successful musicians started by riding busses around the country and playing *gigs*.
  多くの成功したミュージシャンは、バスに乗って国内を回り演奏することから始めた。

Before You Watch

以下は、音楽のジャンルに関する語彙です。1 ～ 12 の空所に当てはまる英語を下のアルファベット表から見つけ、線で囲みましょう。囲み方は縦、横、斜めのいずれも可能です。

例：フォーク　(　folk　)

1. クラシック　(　　)
2. ポップ　(　　)
3. ロック　(　　)
4. ジャズ　(　　)
5. レゲエ　(　　)
6. ヒップホップ　(　　)
7. ラップ　(　　)
8. ソウル　(　　)
9. エレクトロニック　(　　)
10. ブルース　(　　)
11. サンバ　(　　)
12. ディスコ　(　　)

	1	2	3	4	5	6	7	8	9	10	11	12	13	14	15	16
a	F	D	J	G	L	T	R	S	S	D	Q	A	N	J	C	F
b	O	I	H	D	U	E	C	L	A	S	S	I	C	A	L	A
c	L	S	B	I	M	M	R	O	U	M	O	E	L	Z	A	L
d	K	C	L	R	P	O	P	W	L	C	B	U	E	Z	W	S
e	R	O	U	O	A	H	C	R	A	S	I	A	L	A	R	E
f	E	L	E	C	T	R	O	N	I	C	R	E	G	G	A	E
g	J	A	S	K	C	R	O	P	L	O	K	K	N	O	P	B

Watch the News

First Viewing

ニュースを見て、内容と合っているものは T、違っているものは F を選びましょう。

1. ARP's concert tour began in the first year of the Reiwa era. [T / F]

2. Fans can vote for their favorite artist using an application. [T / F]

3. All the characters' voices, movements and facial expressions must be synchronized. [T / F]

Understand the News

Second Viewing

1 ニュースをもう一度見て、各問の空所に入る適切な選択肢をａ～ｃから選びましょう。

1. In back of the stage, you can see ____.

a. English interpreters

b. dancers with motion sensors

c. makeup artists

2. Akari Uchida is ____.

a. a famous videogame creator

b. the owner of this concert hall

c. a former singer and dancer

3. During the two days that ARP performed, they expected an audience of over ____.

a. 300

b. 3,000

c. 30,000

2 右の文字列を並べ替えて単語を作り、各文の空所に入れて意味がとおるようにしましょう。語頭の文字（群）が与えてあるものもあります。

1. This (**c**) of girls came here to see ARP's performance. [dorw]

2. ARP is ( ) for augmented reality performers. [sorht]

3. The reporter must not (**re**) the secret of how these characters can talk with real people. [leva]

4. In ARP's concerts, the shadows are (**v**), not real. [ultair]

3 CD の音声を聞いて、次ページ News Story の❶～❼の文中にある空所に適切な単語を書き入れましょう。音声は２回繰り返されます。 CD 05

● News Story

Narrator: This crowd is here to see a different type of boy band. They are called ARP, short for augmented reality performers. Performances started in 2016, and the fan base is growing.

❶ On top of singing, (　　　[1]) (　　　[2]) (　　　[3]) (　　　[4]) (　　　[5]) (　　　[6]). Part of the reason is because the concerts are **interactive**. Using an **app**, fans can even vote for their favorite member.

❶ 彼らはまた踊ることでも知られている

(*ARP members interact with their fans.*)

But what's behind the excitement? How does it all come together? We've got a special backstage pass to check out the action and find the answers.

❷ Part of the **deal** was we could film as long as we didn't reveal (　　　[1]) (　　　[2]) (　　　[3]) (　　　[4]) (　　　[5]) (　　　[6]). For the group's smooth moves, we saw dancers covered with **motion sensor** technology. ❸ When a dancer moves, (　　　[1]) (　　　[2]) (　　　[3]) (　　　[4]) (　　　[5]).

❷ あるチームメンバーの身元

❸ バンドのメンバーも動く

There are **voice actors** who do the singing and talking. And there are even operators who control facial expressions. ❹ In all, it takes (　　　[1]) (　　　[2]) (　　　[3]) (　　　[4]) (　　　[5]) (　　　[6]) to operate four characters.

❹ ～人以上の高度な訓練を受けたプロ

The group's creator and producer is Akari Uchida, a well known master of creating hit video game series.

***Akari Uchida* (Producer):** ❺ I had the idea of combining the talents of first rate professionals with my characters to create a super-human performer (　　　[1]) (　　　[2]) (　　　[3]) (　　　[4]) (　　　[5])

❺ 現実には存在しない～

([6]) ([7]).

Narrator: ❻ The project's technicians constantly reexamine the performance ([1]) ([2]) ([3]) ([4]) ([5]).

❻ それをもっとリアルにするために

At ARP's concerts even the shadows are virtual and need someone to adjust them.

And it doesn't **matter** how much work goes into characters if their voices, movements and facial expressions are not **synchronized**.

Back on stage, team members are using their skills to entertain a total of 3,600 people over two days.

❼ ARP ([1]) ([2]) ([3]) ([4]) ([5]) ([6]). While they have yet to announce the date for their next **gig**, a public viewing of this concert will be held in April.

❼ これまで～回公演を行ってきた

ARP members: Hello. We are ARP. Please come and see us.

Narrator: Maiko Saito. NHK World.

Review the Key Expressions

各問、選択肢から適切な単語を選び、英文を完成させましょう。なお、余分な単語が１語ずつあります。

1. 消防士に救助された時、その男性は「生きている限りあなたの勇気は忘れません」と言った。

When the man (　　　　　) (　　　　　) by a firefighter, he said, "I will (　　　　　) forget your courage as (　　　　　) (　　　　　) I (　　　　　)."

saved　lived　long　as　live　was　never

2. 洪水で家に大変な被害があった。家を直すには全部で 300 万円かかるかもしれない。

Our house (　　　　　) a (　　　　　) of (　　　　　) because of the (　　　　　). To (　　　　　) the house, it may cost three million yen in (　　　　　).

repair　suffered　flood　damage　lot　all　reform

3. 外国語が流暢になるには、暗記と練習がかなり必要だ。

(　　　　　) (　　　　　) a (　　　　　) of memorization and (　　　　　) to be (　　　　　) in a (　　　　　) language.

practice　it　lot　foreign　much　takes　fluent

4. 若いか年を重ねたかは大した問題じゃないよ。みんなディズニーランドに行くのは好きだよ。

It (　　　　　) (　　　　　) (　　　　　) you are (　　　　　) or old. (　　　　　) loves (　　　　　) to Disneyland.

mind　if　young　going　matter　everyone　doesn't

● Discussion Questions

1. Would you be interested in going to concerts performed by animated characters? Why?

2. What is the name of your favorite anime or manga? Why do you like it? Explain.

UNIT 3

Drinking to Eat

現代人の食事
――「飲む」おにぎり

忙しい現代人にとって、食事のかたちも変化している。「飲む」カレーや「飲む」おにぎりといった新しいタイプの商品が登場しているのだ。缶あるいはパウチ容器入りで、常温保存も可能である。これはどんなに忙しくてもエネルギー補給が必要という人には画期的な商品で、将来的にもそのニーズは多方面にありそうだ。

● Words & Phrases

CD 06

- □ **go-getter** 《口語》やり手、凄腕
- □ **savory** 味のよい、風味のある
- □ **rice ball** おにぎり
- □ to **fly off the shelves** 飛ぶように売れる
  The Nobel Prize winner's book is *flying off the shelves.*
  そのノーベル賞受賞者の本は、飛ぶように売れている。
- □ **texture** 食感、歯ごたえ
- □ **ingredients** 材料、原料
- □ **pickled plums** 梅干し
- □ to **gulp down** ～を飲み込む
- □ to **work on** ～に取り組む
- □ **dietary** 食事の、食に関する
- □ **firmness** 固さ
- □ **viable** 実行可能な
- □ **on the run** 急いで
  Businesspeople are always *on the run.* ビジネスマンはいつも忙しく走り回っている。

Before You Watch

以下は、会話でよく使う慣用的表現です。下の枠内から適切な単語を選び、空所に入れましょう。なお、各語彙１回のみ使えます。また、余分な単語もあります。

1. The new masks are flying off the ( ).［飛ぶように売れる］
2. The test was a piece of ( ).［朝飯前で］
3. Nancy cried her ( ) out because she failed the audition.［泣きはらす］
4. The politician will lose ( ) if he doesn't keep his promise.［めんつを失う］
5. I drank so much at the pub that after I came home, I slept like a ( ).［前後不覚に眠る］
6. Don't be disappointed. Keep your ( ) up!［元気を出す］
7. There's a surprise birthday party for Janet tonight. Don't let the ( ) out of the bag.［秘密をばらす］
8. Hold your ( )! I haven't finished explaining.［あわてるな］
9. I couldn't have said it better. You hit the ( ) on the head.［要点をつく］
10. He wanted to say something at the party, but the cat got his ( ).［黙らせる］

cake	cat	chin	dream	elbows	eyes	face
horses	log	mouse	mud	nail	shelves	tongue

Watch the News First Viewing

ニュースを見て、内容と合っているものはT、違っているものはＦを選びましょう。

1. At a theme park for food, soup curry sales were very good. [T / F]
2. The drinkable rice balls contain grains of rice. [T / F]
3. There are a lot of favorable reviews about the drinkable rice balls. [T / F]

Understand the News　　Second Viewing

1 ニュースをもう一度見て、各問の空所に入る適切な選択肢をa～cから選びましょう。

1. ____ included in the liquid curry made by a mail order company.

a. Every ingredient except meat is
b. All the necessary ingredients are
c. Some vegetables, such as carrots, are not

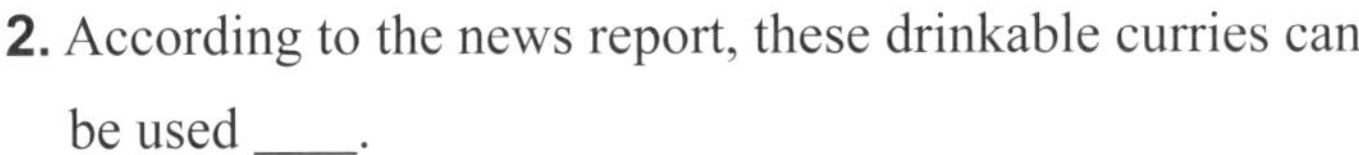

2. According to the news report, these drinkable curries can be used ____.

a. as food during emergencies
b. at nursing homes
c. for children's breakfasts

3. The reporter had ____ in her bag.

a. a can of drinkable curry and a jelly dessert
b. drinkable rice balls and pickled plums
c. a drinkable *onigiri* pouch and drinkable curry

2 右の文字列を並べ替えて単語を作り、各文の空所に入れて意味がとおるようにしましょう。

1. Drinkable meals are (　　　　　　　) foods, and they are becoming popular in Japan. [qduili]
2. Drinkable rice balls have hit the (　　　　　　　) recently. [mretak]
3. The company selling drinkable meals targets busy (　　　　　　　)people. [sensbuis]
4. Customers enjoy not only the taste but the (　　　　　　　) of *onigiri*. [erxtetu]

3 CDの音声を聞いて、次ページNews Storyの❶～❼の文中にある空所に適切な単語を書き入れましょう。音声は2回繰り返されます。 CD 07

● News Story

Reporter: ❶ Our next story is from Japan, a country ([1]) ([2]) ([3]) ([4]) ([5]) ([6]) and busy way of life. So, the latest trend in food? A rise in drinkable meals. As many **go-getters** are eager to finish eating quickly to return to their desks, companies are developing nutritious and **savory** liquid foods. Let's take a look.

❶ 利便性が大好きなことで知られている

Narrator: ❷ At a theme park for food, one product ([1]) ([2]) ([3]) ([4]) ([5]) ([6]), drinkable **rice balls**. They hit the market in Japan in March. Sales have been beyond expectations with more than two million packets **flying off the shelves** so far.

❷ 多くの注目を集めている

Rice grains can be seen in the liquid. The maker says it tried to maintain the **texture** of rice while turning other **ingredients**, such as seaweed and **pickled plums**, into jelly form.

The firm originally developed the drinkable rice balls for busy businesspeople. It wanted them to have a quick way to eat in their offices or while commuting. ❸ But people have gone beyond that and ([1]) ([2]) ([3]) ([4]) ([5]) ([6]) the outdoors and on hiking trips. There's been a flood of positive comments online.

❸ 食事を〜に持って行っている

Shingo Inotani (Manager, Konnyaku Park): People say they enjoy the taste and texture. They say *it's**[1] just like real rice balls.

Narrator: Another company has made a drink out of a dish that people usually sit down to eat as a full meal. It's drinkable curry made by a mail order company. Last year they put about 4,000 cans on the market as a trial. They sold out immediately. A remark by an employee at a product-planning session inspired the development.

They said that when they're busy, they drink, heat and eat curry straight from the packet. Others said that they did the same thing. ❹ And so the company thought that ([1]) ([2]) ([3]) ([4]) ([5]) ([6]) a drinkable curry.

❹ ～の需要があるかもしれない

The liquid curry contains all the ingredients from meat to vegetables. It's easy to **gulp down** and still has curry's rich taste. ❺ The can is designed to be easy for people ([1]) ([2]) ([3]) ([4]) ([5]), ([6]). After the trial's success, the firm is now **working on** other variations. One is a Thai curry.

❺ どこでも、いつでもカレーを飲むこと

***Kazuhiko Yazaki** (President and CEO, Felissimo):* We're working on many types of curries and changing them so they are drinkable. ❻ There are ([1]) ([2]) ([3]) ([4]) ([5]) ([6]) in this **dietary** field.

❻ やるべき、多くの新しい挑戦（がある）

Narrator: Customers are saying that the curries are easy to drink and are full of good spices. These drinkable meals could find many uses, including becoming a part of emergency supply kits. This new world of food may *only**[2] be just starting to heat up.

Reporter: ❼ Look at ([1]) ([2]) ([3]) ([4]) ([5]) ([6]) today. Yes, the drinkable curry and *onigiri* rice ball. I opened an *onigiri* pouch earlier. Though it's not the real thing, I found all the familiar aromas of Japan's famous snack, and the grains of rice had a pleasant **firmness**, so it may be a **viable** choice for a person **on the run**.

❼ 私が詰めて（もって）きたもの

Notes

*[1] it's は、口語では複数のものを指す場合でもよく使う

*[2] early のように聞こえるが only が正しい

Review the Key Expressions

各問、選択肢から適切な単語を選び、英文を完成させましょう。なお、余分な単語が１語ずつあります。

1. 彼らが用意した興行は、本人たちの予想をはるかに超える大成功だった。

The ( ) that they ( ) was a ( ) ( ), far ( ) their ( ).

big provided way beyond entertainment expectations success

2. 政治スキャンダルが明るみに出るとすぐに、一般市民からあふれるほどの問い合わせや不満が押し寄せた。

As ( ) as the political scandal was ( ), there was a ( ) of ( ) and complaints from ( ) ( ).

citizens revealed soon flood came private inquires

3. 日米の文化の違いに興味があるって言っていましたね。今書いている［手がけている］論文はそれに関係があるのですか。

You said you are ( ) in the ( ) ( ) ( ) America and Japan. Is the ( ) that you are ( ) on ( ) to that?

paper interested involved related differences between cultural working

4. 健太は雑談する時間さえもない 。バイトを２つ掛け持ちしていて、いつも忙しい。

Kenta ( ) has ( ) to ( ). He has two ( ) jobs and is always ( ) the ( ).

on part-time run never time out chat

● Discussion Questions

1. Would you be interested in pouched liquid meals, such as curry or *onigiri*? Why or why not?

2. Do you think people have to work harder today than they did 30 years ago? If yes, why do you think so? If no, why not?

UNIT 4 Next Generation Mobility

次世代の移動手段

東京モーターショーは世界5大モーターショーの一つで、車に関する最新技術やデザインの情報を発信する見本市である。最新の自動運転技術は自動車メーカーだけではなく、様々な異業種の分野で応用が期待されている。より便利で安全な社会の構築は永遠の課題であり、日本の技術力の高さが体感できる場となった。

● Words & Phrases

CD 08

- ☐ to **take on**　〜を引き受ける
- ☐ **automotive industry**　自動車産業
- ☐ **autonomous**　自律性の
- ☐ to **make a push**　努力する
- ☐ **drone**　ドローン
- ☐ **agricultural produce**　農作物
- ☐ **steering wheel**　ハンドル
- ☐ **an array of**　ずらりと並んだ〜
  Department stores carry *an array of* stylish handbags every season.
  デパートは毎シーズン、スタイリッシュなハンドバッグをずらりと並べて販売している。
- ☐ **pedestrian**　歩行者
- ☐ to **dwindle**　しだいに減少する
- ☐ to **make the rounds**　巡回する
  The police are *making the rounds* in the most dangerous neighborhoods this evening.
  警察は今晩、最も危険な地域を巡回している。

Before You Watch

以下は、車関係の英語表現です。下の枠内から適切な単語［米語］を選び、空所に入れましょう。なお、余分な単語もあります。

1. ハンドル　steering (　　　　　)
2. バックミラー　(　　　　　)-view mirror
3. フロントガラス　(　　　　　)
4. ナンバープレート　(　　　　　) plate
5. ガソリンスタンド　gas (　　　　　)
6. サイドブレーキ　(　　　　　) brake
7. アクセル　(　　　　　) pedal
8. パンク　(　　　　　) tire
9. オープンカー　(　　　　　)
10. クラクション　(　　　　　)
11. ボンネット　(　　　　　)
12. ウィンカー　(　　　　　) signal
13. 高速道路　(　　　　　)

bypath	convertible	flat	freeway	gas	hood
horn	license	parking	rear	service	side
spike	station	turn	wheel	windshield	

Watch the News　First Viewing

ニュースを見て、内容と合っているものはT、違っているものはFを選びましょう。

1. This motor show centered around self-driving technology. [T / F]
2. Robocar® Walk is equipped with a touch screen, not a steering wheel. [T / F]
3. Robocar® Walk is designed exclusively to help Japanese and English speakers. [T / F]

Understand the News　　Second Viewing

1 ニュースをもう一度見て、各問の空所に入る適切な選択肢をａ～ｃから選びましょう。

1. This autonomous land drone is designed to ____.
  a. help farmers trim grass
  b. carry farm products
  c. function as a stool for people to sit on

2. Robocar® Walk ____.
  a. can go six kilometers per hour at its fastest
  b. is operated with a handle bar and a pedal
  c. always runs on regular roads and streets

3. At airports, Robocar® Walk helps ____.
  a. people who don't have a driver's license
  b. people who carry a lot of suitcases
  c. senior citizens and injured people

2 以下の各情報を、ニュースに出てきた順序に並べましょう。

1. A land drone has been developed to help farmers.
2. Robocar® Walk stops and talks to people who are in its way.
3. Autonomous carts deliver food and drinks to you.
4. Robocar® Walk follows the traffic rules and observes signals.

3 CD の音声を聞いて、次ページ News Story の❶～❼の文中にある空所に適切な単語を書き入れましょう。音声は２回繰り返されます。　CD 09

● News Story

Anchor: This year's Tokyo Motor Show is **taking on** the most recent trend in the **automotive industry**, and that's **autonomous** driving technology. The high tech *concept**1 also doesn't stop with the major automakers. ❶ It's being (1) (2) (3) (4) (5) (6). NHK World's John LaDue has checked out the latest inventions.

❶ 様々な分野で利用されて

Reporter (John LaDue): At this month's Tokyo Motor Show, autonomous mobility took center stage as the auto industry **makes a push** toward driverless tech. This self-driving taxi on display has interactive digital windows and a roof for rider entertainment.

The new mobility is not just for passenger vehicles either. This is an autonomous land **drone** being developed to move **agricultural produce** from farm field to warehouse.

❷ Autonomous carts could soon (1) (2), (3) (4) (5) (6) wherever you are.

❷ 郵便や小包や食物を届ける

And welcome to the world of robot mobility. This is called Robocar® Walk. The vehicle doesn't have a **steering wheel** or pedals. Passengers just choose where they want to go on a touch screen, and the device does the rest. ❸ It stops when the crosswalk signal is red and continues on its journey (1) (2) (3) (4) (5).

❸ 信号が青［緑］になると

The robot uses **an array of** cameras and sensors to navigate sidewalks at speeds of up to six kilometers an hour.

There are a lot of **pedestrians** on their smartphones walking these days, so if I with my smartphone come in front of Robocar® Walk, it notices me, and it says kindly, ...

Robocar: Excuse me. Could you please let us pass?

Reporter: I get out of its way. Robocar® Walk... goes on its way.

This technology comes as Japan's aging population and **dwindling** number of taxi and bus drivers create*s**[2] a growing need for new solutions. ❹ The vehicle is already **making the rounds** at airports, (　　　[1]) (　　　[2]) (　　　[3]) (　　　[4]) (　　　[5]) (　　　[6]) get to their flight gates on time.

❹ 年配者やけががをしている乗客を助けながら

(*The reporter gets in the Robocar® Walk.*) So, I get inside.

Its creators are also programing it to be a guide for foreign tourists, just as Tokyo prepares to host next year's Olympic and Paralympic Games. ❺ The device (　　　[1]) (　　　[2]) (　　　[3]) (　　　[4]) (　　　[5]) (　　　[6]) with passengers in multiple languages.

❺ いずれはお話をすることができるだろう

Just me and my Robocar. (*The reporter talks to the Robocar® Walk.*) Hey, Robocar, do you see, you see that over there?

Hisashi Taniguchi **_(Founder & CEO, ZMP):_** ❻ There are many elderly people in Japan who can't walk long distances and with the driver shortage, we can expect there will be (　　　[1]) (　　　[2]) (　　　[3]) (　　　[4]) (　　　[5]) (　　　[6]) (　　　[7]).

❻ この種の仕事の需要が大幅に増える

Reporter: ❼ Autonomous technology (　　　[1]) (　　　[2]) (　　　[3]) (　　　[4]) (　　　[5]) (　　　[6]). It's a change that has a potential to solve current problems while taking us to new and unexpected places. John LaDue, NHK World, Tokyo.

❼ 移動性の概念を変えている

Notes

*[1] 語尾に [s] のような摩擦音が聞こえるが、不要

*[2] 文法的に -s は不要だが、くだけた会話では普通

Review the Key Expressions

各問、選択肢から適切な単語を選び、英文を完成させましょう。なお、余分な単語が1語ずつあります。

1. 由衣は先生としてのボランティア経験を生かして、大学の講師になった。

Yui ( ) her ( ) experience ( ) a teacher ( ) ( ) and ( ) a university instructor.

use as living volunteer to became put

2. 合衆国と中国はこれから何年も、世界経済の首脳会談で中心的役割を担うと思われている。

It is ( ) that the USA and China will ( ) ( ) ( ) at world ( ) ( ) for many years to ( ).

summits believed center throw come stage economic take

3. その日本の家電メーカーは、中国との競争に加わるため最近大きな頑張りをみせている。

The Japanese electrical ( ) manufacturer ( ) recently ( ) a big ( ) to ( ) into ( ) with China.

enter appliance push has competition hold made

4. 企業は読みやすい時計など、年配者のために新しい製品をデザインしている。

( ) are ( ) new ( ) for ( ) ( ), such ( ) easy-to-read watches.

people products companies as designing like elderly

● Discussion Questions

1. Should people use public transportation rather than driving cars? State your opinion and reasons.

2. Would you be interested in buying a driverless automobile in the future? Why or why not?

UNIT 5

Eco-friendly Fashion Statement

衣料品ロス
—— 名前を変えて

衣料品の余剰在庫廃棄処分が大きな社会問題となっている。特にブランド会社はそのイメージを確保するために売れ残った商品を廉価で販売するわけにはいかない。こうした中、新しい販売スタイルが注目を集めている。余った商品を無駄にすることなく新たな価値を与えて販売している、ある企業の取り組みをレポートする。

● Words & Phrases

CD 10

- ☐ **eco-friendly**　環境にやさしい
- ☐ to **come up with**　～を思いつく
- ☐ **garment**　衣服〈主に商業用語〉
- ☐ **irresponsible**　無責任な
- ☐ **exclusivity**　独占性〈ここでは「特別であること」や「高級なイメージ」を意味する〉
- ☐ **fix**　《米略式》解決法
  There is no quick *fix* for this problem.
  この問題にすばやい解決法などない。
- ☐ to **snip off**　～を切り落とす
  She *snipped off* the dead leaves from the tree.
  彼女はその木から枯葉を切り落とした。
- ☐ **tag**　タグ、襟づり
- ☐ to **rebadge**　新しい名前で再発売する
- ☐ **rallying cry**　（政治運動などの）スローガン
- ☐ **apparel**　アパレル、衣服

Before You Watch

以下は、環境問題に関する表現です。下の枠内から適切な単語を選び、空所に入れましょう。

1. これらの環境にやさしいバッグは生分解性［微生物によって分解される］プラスチックでできている。
These eco-friendly bags are made of (   ) plastics.

2. 環境にやさしい製品に人気が出てきた。
Environmentally-friendly or (   ) products have become popular.

3. 私たちは環境的に持続可能なライフスタイルを選ぶべきだ。
We should adopt an environmentally (   ) lifestyle.

4. この授業では、地球温暖化や熱帯雨林の破壊などの環境問題に焦点を当てる。
This class will focus on environmental issues such as (   ) (   ) and the (   ) of our rain forests.

5. 人々は温室効果ガスの排出を削減するため、公共交通機関を使うよう促されている。
People are encouraged to use (   ) transportation to reduce (   ) gas emissions.

6. 使い捨てのプラスチックストローは、環境に配慮したものに代えられるべきだ。
(   ) plastic straws should be replaced by eco-friendly alternatives.

7. 車の排気ガスは健康を害する大気汚染を引き起こす。
(   ) from motor vehicles cause air (   ), known to be harmful to your health.

biodegradable	destruction	emissions	global	green	greenhouse
pollution	public	single-use	sustainable	warming	

Watch the News

First Viewing

ニュースを見て、内容と合っているものはT、違っているものはFを選びましょう。

1. Tens of millions of dollars' worth of clothes are disposed of every year. [T / F]

2. Discarding unused clothes has become a world problem. [T / F]

3. Instead of throwing clothes away, selling them is an environmentally better solution. [T / F]

Understand the News　　Second Viewing

1 ニュースをもう一度見て、各問の空所に入る適切な選択肢を a ～ c から選びましょう。

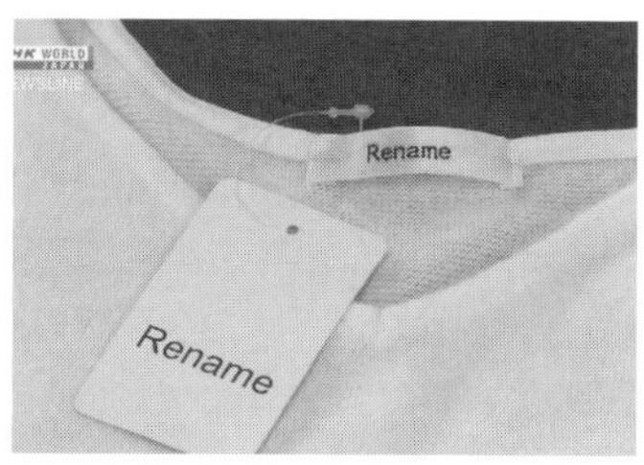

1. Rename started in ____.
  a. Tokyo in 2016
  b. central Japan last year
  c. Nagoya over three years ago

2. The CEO thought if the original brand was not shown on the clothes, ____.
  a. her company could not sell the products
  b. her company had to sell them at the same price
  c. the clothing could be sold with different labels

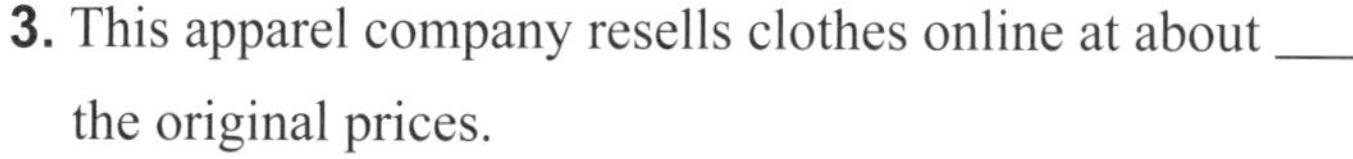

3. This apparel company resells clothes online at about ____ the original prices.
  a. 30 percent off
  b. 70 percent off
  c. 70 percent of

2 右の文字列を並べ替えて単語を作り、各文の空所に入れて意味がとおるようにしましょう。語頭の文字が与えてあるものもあります。

1. The word (**g**) originates from French and means “a piece of clothing.” [netamr]

2. Rename is tackling a waste problem in the (**f**) industry. [hinaos]

3. Clothing waste has become a (**g**) issue recently. [blola]

4. Customers of Rename buy clothing ( ). [eilnon]

3 CD の音声を聞いて、次ページ News Story の❶～❼の文中にある空所に適切な単語を書き入れましょう。音声は２回繰り返されます。 CD 11

● News Story

Anchor: It's one of fashion's worst kept secrets. Every year companies destroy millions of dollars' worth of unsold clothes. They say it's a way to protect their brands. But as our next story shows, a Japanese business has **come up with** a way to address their concerns while insuring the **garments** don't go to waste.

Narrator: ❶ Boxes and boxes of new, name brand clothing: (　　　　[1]) (　　　　[2]) (　　　　[3]) (　　　　[4]) (　　　　[5]) (　　　　[6]) using a different label. Rename started in Nagoya in 2016. The firm is trying to combat high levels of waste in the fashion industry.

❶ その全部が生まれ変わるだろう

❷ CEO Yukari Kato remembers being shocked when she found out (　　　　[1]) (　　　　[2]) (　　　　[3]) (　　　　[4]) (　　　　[5]) (　　　　[6]).

❷ 製造業者が衣料をどれだけ廃棄しているか

Yukari Kato (CEO, FINE): ❸ I would often speak to clothing brands about how **irresponsible** it is, especially (　　　　[1]) (　　　　[2]) (　　　　[3]) (　　　　[4]) (　　　　[5]) (　　　　[6]).

❸ 衣料品は腐ったりしないので

Narrator: The issue has been a global talking point in recent years. Some firms admitted to destroying stock rather than selling it cheaply to protect the **exclusivity** of their brands.

Kato: Most companies worry that if they sell clothing bearing their label, they'll have no control over where and how it's sold. ❹ They think it's better (　　　　[1]) (　　　　[2]) (　　　　[3]) (　　　　[4]) (　　　　[5]) (　　　　[6]). My idea was if the brand is invisible, the clothing could be used like any other product.

❹ それを単に処分する

Narrator: It's an easy **fix**. Workers simply **snip off** the original **tags** and replace them with these. That way customers don't know what the original brand was. ❺ The company counts the old tags and returns them to the manufacturers to reassure them that

❺ 彼らの評価が影響を受けていない

(1) (2) (3) (4) (5).

The process is much the same for clothing care labels. ❻ If they mention the brand, workers cut them out and replace them, making sure to include (1) (2) (3) (4) (5) (6) the garment.

❻ ～を手入れする方法の説明

On busy days, the company **rebadges** roughly 200 items of clothing. It sells the clothes online at about 30 percent of their original price. Over the past two years, the firm has sold roughly 250,000 items. It's good for the environment and good for customers' peace of mind.

Kato: ❼ I want to build on what we're doing by showing people that (1) (2) (3) (4) (5) (6) (7). It's helping the planet.

❼ 彼らの購入が楽しい経験というだけではない

Narrator: Thanks to the initiative of Kato and others like her, recycling is fast becoming a **rallying cry** throughout the **apparel** industry.

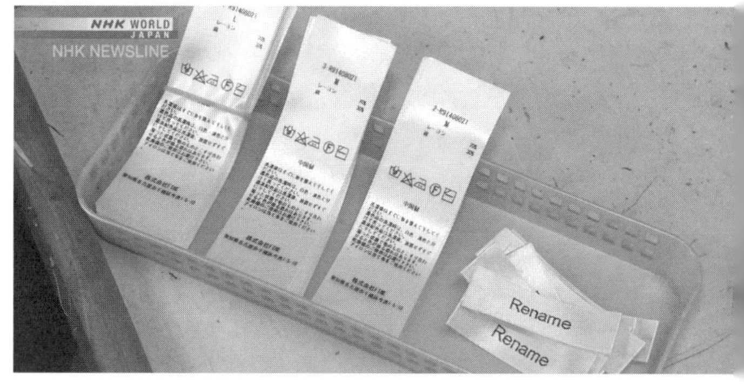

Review the Key Expressions

各問、選択肢から適切な単語を選び、英文を完成させましょう。なお、余分な単語が１語ずつあります。

1. 世界中で、新型コロナウイルスに効くワクチンを見つけた［思いついた］研究班はありますか。

( ) ( ) research team in the world ( ) ( ) ( ) a coronavirus ( )?

up has get come vaccine with any

2. 首都警察は、その交通事故がどのようにして起きたか解明しようと懸命になっている。

The metropolitan police are ( ) very hard to ( ) ( ) ( ) the ( ) ( ) happened.

at out traffic trying find accident how

3. 会議に来るように求められていたのに、義務を怠るなんて彼も無責任だ。

He ( ) ( ) to come to the meeting. It was ( ) of ( ) to ( ) his ( ).

neglect required irresponsible him irresistible was duties

4. 研究者や医師のたゆまぬ努力のおかげで、結核による死者数が劇的に減少した。

( ) ( ) the ( ) efforts of researchers and doctors, the ( ) of ( ) from tuberculosis has dramatically ( ).

to number decreased thanks untiring deaths increased

● Discussion Questions

1. What do you think of Rename's idea and business style? Explain.

2. What can people do to contribute to an eco-friendly society?

UNIT 6 Building a Bridge to Share a Son's Dream

日韓の架け橋になりたい

悲劇は 2001 年 1 月に起こった。JR 新大久保駅で、ある男性が線路に転落した。勇敢にも韓国からの留学生が他の日本人とともに救助に向かった。しかし運悪く 3 人とも車両にはねられ亡くなってしまった。その後不備だった足場やホームの防護壁の設置が始まり、日韓関係を好転させる大きな契機にもなった。

● Words & Phrases

CD 12

- □ **track**　線路
- □ **outpouring**　〈感情などの〉ほとばしり
- □ **fraught**　緊張した
  Before the press conference, the prime minister had a *fraught* expression on his face.
  記者会見の前に首相は緊張した表情を浮かべた。
- □ **memorial**　追悼式典
- □ **gratitude**　感謝
- □ **condolence money**　弔慰金（ちょういきん）
- □ to **screen**　～を上映する
- □ to **endure**　〈困難や苦痛など〉に耐える
- □ **late**　故、亡くなった
  The show was dedicated to the *late* TV personality who died of pneumonia.
  その番組は肺炎で亡くなったテレビタレントに捧げられた。
- □ to **transcend**　～を越える

Before You Watch

以下は、人間関係に関する記述です。下の枠内から適切な表現を選び、空所に入れましょう。なお、余分な単語もあります。

1. 私は上司とは良い関係だ。　I have a good relationship with my ( ).

2. 職場の人たちとうまくいっていない。
I have trouble ( ) ( ) with people at my workplace.

3. 他の人たちに思いやりを持つべきだ。
You should have some ( ) for other people.

4. ストレスの一般的な原因は仕事と人間関係である。
( ) ( ) of stress are work and human relationships.

5. 新しい隣人たちと私はすぐに仲良くなった。
The new neighbors and I ( ) immediately.

6. スーザンとジェイソンは恋愛関係にある。
Susan and Jason are in a ( ) relationship.

7. 学校でいじめに苦しんでいる学生が多い。
There are many students ( ) by ( ) at school.

8. 彼は新人にきびしい。　He is ( ) on the new employees.

9. 私には良い同僚がいて本当に運が良い。
I'm really lucky to have good ( ).

along	boss	bullying	common	concentration	
consideration	coworkers	easy	fellow	getting	hard
hit it off	recruit	romantic	sources	troubled	

Watch the News　First Viewing

ニュースを見て、内容と合っているものはT、違っているものはFを選びましょう。

1. Shin recently attended a memorial service for her son. [T / F]

2. Before Lee Su-hyun was killed in the accident, he had known a lot of people in Japan. [T / F]

3. Shin's husband passed away before this year's memorial. [T / F]

Understand the News　　Second Viewing

1 ニュースをもう一度見て、各問の空所に入る適切な選択肢をａ～ｃから選びましょう。

1. Lee Su-hyun was interested in finding a job in ____.
a. selling and buying merchandise
b. teaching Korean to Japanese people
c. tourism between the two countries

2. The condolence money was used for ____.
a. repairing facilities at the JR station
b. helping foreign students to learn Japanese
c. remodeling the Japanese school

3. Shin plans to ____.
a. keep working for mutual understanding between Korea and Japan
b. move to Japan and teach Korean to Japanese people
c. open a trading company in the Korean Town in the Shin-okubo area

2 以下はニュースの概要です。空所に適切な単語を書き入れましょう。語頭の文字(群)は与えてあります。

A student from South Korea, Lee Su-hyun, tried to help a Japanese who fell down on the (**t** [1]) at a train station. Unfortunately, all three men involved in the accident lost their lives. But people honored Lee's brave actions and his contribution as a (**b** [2]) between Korea and Japan. After the (**tr** [3]) Lee's father and mother started visiting Japan and helped people set up a (**sc** [4]). A movie was also made about Lee's bravery. Although his father died this year, his mother is determined to continue coming to Japan to make her son's (**d** [5]) come true.

3 CD の音声を聞いて、次ページ News Story の❶～❼の文中にある空所に適切な単語を書き入れましょう。音声は２回繰り返されます。　CD 13

● News Story

Anchor: In 2001 a South Korean student in Japan saw a man fall to the **tracks** at a busy train station. He immediately jumped down to help, but lost his life in the effort. ❶ An **outpouring** of emotion seemed to ([1]) ([2]) ([3]) ([4]) ([5]) ([6]). His mother is keeping her son's hopes of bridging the two nations alive, 18 years after his death despite **fraught** relations.

❶ その2つの国をより親密にする

Narrator: ❷ Shin Yoon-chan ([1]) ([2]) ([3]) ([4]) ([5]) in Tokyo where there's a **memorial** to her son. In 2001 her son Lee Su-hyun was studying Japanese there so he could find a job at a trading company and be a bridge between South Korea and Japan.

❷ 最近その語学学校を訪問した

❸ The ([1]) ([2]) ([3]) ([4]) ([5]) ([6]) expressing sympathy and **gratitude**.

❸ 家族は日本から数え切れないほどの手紙を受け取った

***Shin Yoon-chan** (Lee Su-hyun's mother):* ❹ He was a foreign student in Japan and didn't know many people yet, so we are very thankful that ([1]) ([2]) ([3]) ([4]) ([5]) ([6]) ([7]). We are determined to do our best to fulfill his wish.

❹ かなり多くの人たちが私たちに寄り添おうとしてくれた

Narrator: ❺ After the tragedy, Lee's parents began visiting Japan to talk about the ([1]) ([2]) ([3]) ([4]) ([5]) ([6]), regardless of nationality.

❺ お互いに相手を思いやることの大切さ

They used the **condolence money** they received to set up a scholarship for people who want to study Japanese, just like their son.

Shin: The scholarship makes me feel like I have many children.

Lee Sung-dae (Lee Su-hyun's father): I want them to make their dreams come true, for themselves and for my son.

Narrator: A 2017 documentary about their son titled *I Am a Bridge!* *1 has been **screened** around Japan.

Lee Sung-dae: (*He comments in the documentary.*) There is nothing we can say to each other having lost our son. We can only **endure** our pain in silence.

Student from South Korea: ❻ I hope ([1]) ([2]) ([3]) ([4]) ([5]) ([6]) ([7]) and the next.

❻ 私たちの絆が今の世代で継続する

Narrator: This year Shin *had lost**2 her husband who usually made the trip with her. Shin visited the site of the accident alone.

Shin: (*On the platform of the accident site*) I feel like my son is always here, watching over me. ❼ I'll keep doing all I can, so ([1]) ([2]) ([3]) ([4]) ([5]) ([6]).

❼ 彼の言いたいことが忘れられてしまうことがない

Narrator: Shin plans to continue her efforts, believing like her **late** son and husband, that bonds between people **transcend** borders.

Notes

*1 2001年に起きたこの事故を題材にしたドキュメンタリー映画『かけはし』

*2 過去形のlostが正しい

Review the Key Expressions

各問、選択肢から適切な単語を選び、英文を完成させましょう。なお、余分な単語が 1 語ずつあります。

1. 若い力士が亡くなった後、彼の多くのファンから深い悲しみが次々と寄せられた。

( ) the young sumo ( ) ( ), an ( ) of ( ) came ( ) his many fans.

grief from wrestler's outpouring death after passed

2. チャンピオンは、シーズン最後の競技でベストを尽くすと決めた。

The champion ( ) ( ) to ( ) ( ) ( ) in her last ( ) of the season.

do was best defeated competition determined her

3. 彼についていろいろ思うことがあるかもしれないけれど、彼は本当に信頼できる政治家です。

( ) ( ) what you ( ) ( ) about him, he is ( ) a ( ) politician.

trustworthy of regarding truly may think regardless

4. 大坂なおみはウィンブルドン大会優勝に向けてすべての努力をつぎ込んで、その夢を実現させた。

Naomi Osaka ( ) all her ( ) into ( ) the Wimbledon championship and ( ) her dream ( ) ( ).

effort come fulfill put true made winning

● Discussion Questions

1. Who is/are your true hero(es) or heroine(s)? Explain why.

2. What are your dreams regarding your future job, family, wealth or life in general? Explain.

UNIT 7 Taking Aim

シュートの達人
――スリーポイントおじいさん

沖縄県宜野湾市に、バスケの「スリーポイントシュート」対決で勝ち続ける伝説のおじいさんがいる。宮城善光さんは独立リーグのプロ選手にも勝利し、その動画がネットで公開されるなど話題を呼んでいる。常に勝負に挑むのは、米軍基地が集中する沖縄で生まれ育った故の特別な思い入れがその背景にあるという。

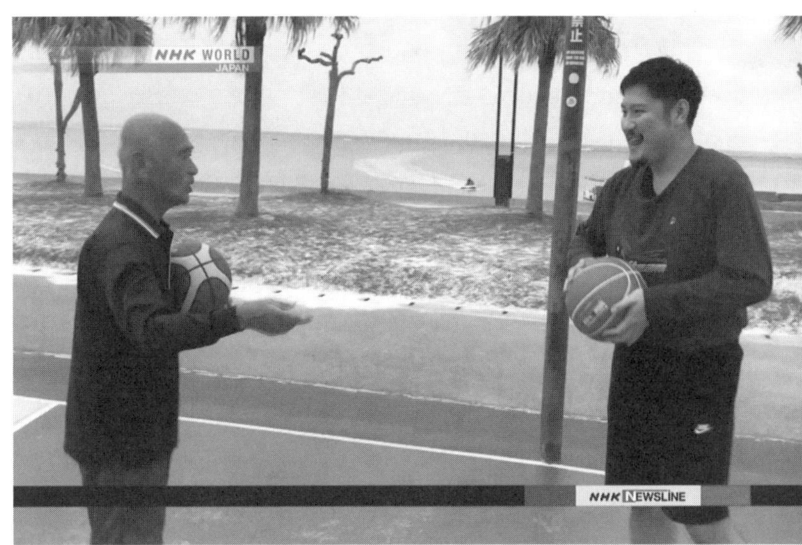

● Words & Phrases

CD 14

- □ **three-pointer** 《バスケット》3点シュートを決める選手
- □ **pension** 年金
- □ **whiz** 《口語》達人、名手
- □ to **drain baskets** シュートを決める
- □ to **go viral** （ネットで）拡散する、急速に広がる
  The video of a policeman killing a black man *went viral*.
  警察官が黒人男性を殺害するビデオが拡散した。
- □ to **compensate for** ～を補う
- □ to **launch** ～を投げ出す
- □ **hoop** 《バスケット》ゴール
- □ **workaholic** 《口語》仕事中毒の
- □ to **confiscate** ～を没収する
- □ **contender** 競争相手
- □ **independent league** 独立リーグ
- □ **showdown** 対決
- □ **wizard** 《口語》名人
- □ to **hone** 〈能力など〉に磨きをかける
  Watch English news regularly to *hone* your listening skills.
  リスニングのスキルに磨きをかけるためには、定期的に英語のニュースを見なさい。

Before You Watch

ニュースには workaholic や independent のような複数の形態素で成り立っている語彙が出てきます。以下は語源に関する問題です。下線部の意味を下の枠内から選び、空所に入れましょう。なお、余分な選択肢もあります。

1. workaholic, chocoholic ( )
2. independent, suspend ( )
3. decade, decathlon ( )
4. democracy, pandemic ( )

5. percent, century ( )
6. pedal, pedestrian ( )
7. bicycle, bilingual ( )
8. describe, manuscript ( )

9. triangle, triple ( )
10. manual, manufacture ( )
11. suicide, insecticide ( )
12. postpone, postscript ( )

後ろに	垂れる	～中毒の	感謝	輪	書く	手	
人々	自分	～殺し	足	置く	前に	言語の	全体の
1	2	3	10	100	1,000		

Watch the News
First Viewing

ニュースを見て、内容と合っているものは T、違っているものは F を選びましょう。

1. Miyagi has taken on three-point shoot challenges from hundreds of people. [T / F]
2. Three-point shoots are made from a point over six meters away from the hoop. [T / F]
3. Miyagi's land was taken away by the US military over 100 years ago. [T / F]

Understand the News　Second Viewing

1 ニュースをもう一度見て、各問の空所に入る適切な選択肢をa～cから選びましょう。

1. Miyagi started practicing basketball ____.
  a. when he was in his late 20s
  b. after World War II ended in 1945
  c. a quarter of a century or so ago

2. Matsuda ____.
  a. came all the way from the US to see Miyagi in person
  b. is a professional basketball player in the US
  c. played against Miyagi and won one game out of four

3. Miyagi is hoping for the day when he ____.
  a. is invited to the US to show off his technique
  b. will win 500 three-pointer competitions
  c. can take on a legendary American player

2 以下はニュースの概要です。空所に適切な単語を書き入れましょう。語頭の文字(群)は与えてあります。

Zenko Miyagi is an (**el** [1]) man in his mid-70s living in Okinawa. He is very good at shooting hoops outside the (**t** [2])-point line. He has won a lot of competitions even with (**pr** [3]) basketball players. In 500 games, he has never lost to an American (**con** [4]). He had a bad experience with the US military when they took away his (**l** [5]). He wants to get (**re** [6]) by winning these basketball matches. He really wants to have a (**sh** [7]) with Michael Jordan, the "God of basketball" some time.

3 CDの音声を聞いて、次ページNews Storyの❶～❼の文中にある空所に適切な単語を書き入れましょう。音声は2回繰り返されます。 CD 15

● News Story

Anchor: You'd probably expect the best basketball **three-pointers** to be made by players who are athletic and young, but one celebrated sharp shooter from southern Japan is old enough to be collecting his **pension**. We meet the elderly basketball **whiz** who's taken on hundreds of challengers.

Narrator: An older man in a three-pointer contest, scoring one goal after another: A video of him **draining baskets went viral** on the Internet.

Man 1: I officially lost?

Zenko Miyagi: ❶ I'm nervous because ([1]) ([2]) ([3]) ([4]) ([5]) ([6]).

❶ カメラには慣れていないのです

Narrator: The three point specialist is 74-year-old Zenko Miyagi. He fires the ball in from outside the three-point line, a distance of over six meters. Miyagi is only one meter 63 tall, but he **compensates for** his lack of height with an unusual technique, **launching** his whole body into the shot.

Miyagi: ❷ I practice about 340 days a year unless ([1]) ([2]) ([3]) ([4]) ([5]) ([6]) ([7]). It's important to keep practicing.

❷ 何か用事［私を近づけないもの］がある

Narrator: Miyagi was over 50 years old when he started shooting **hoops**. ❸ He wanted an escape from his **workaholic** lifestyle, ([1]) ([2]) ([3]) ([4]) ([5]) ([6]).

❸ でも、それが唯一の動機ではなかった

His family had owned land in Okinawa for many generations. But in 1945 it was **confiscated** by the US military and used to build a base for the Marines. To get his own back, he wanted to perfect an American sport and get so good at it that he could beat players from America.

Miyagi: Can you hear all the loud noise? ❹ It goes on all day long, even at times of day when (　　　[1]) (　　　[2]) (　　　[3]) (　　　[4]) (　　　[5]) (　　　[6]) (　　　[7]). I had this feeling of, "*Damn you*,*[1] America!" and I wanted to beat them somehow, like through basketball.

❹ 人々がくつろいでテレビを見たい

Narrator: Miyagi has now beaten 500 American **contenders** in a row.

Kouki Matsuda is a professional basketball player for an **independent league** in the US. He's in Okinawa for a training camp. He and Miyagi start battling it out to see who can score ten hoops first. The professional Matsuda wants to do himself proud. ❺ But (　　　[1]) (　　　[2]) (　　　[3]) (　　　[4]) (　　　[5]) (　　　[6]), and Miyagi is sinking basket after basket.

❺ 自分が思った［望んだ］ようにいっていない

Miyagi: ❻ (　　　[1]) (　　　[2]) (　　　[3]) (　　　[4]) (　　　[5]) (　　　[6]).

❻ 今日は私のほうにツキがありました

Narrator: They played five games and Miyagi won four of them.

Kouki Matsuda: It was frustrating, so frustrating and amazing. He may not have a beautiful style, but you shoot to score. The results say it all.

Narrator: ❼ Miyagi has a long held dream, to take on the player (　　　[1]) (　　　[2]) (　　　[3]) (　　　[4]) (　　　[5]) (　　　[6]) (　　　[7]).

❼ よく、史上最高と言われる

Miyagi: If I competed against *Michael Jordan**[2] on three-pointers, I would definitely win.

Narrator: For Miyagi, victory against Jordan would be symbolic revenge for the wrong done to him decades ago. Until that **showdown** happens, the three-point **wizard** continues to **hone** his skills one hoop at a time.

Notes　＊[1] Damn you は口語で、相手を罵る言葉「こんちくしょう」　＊[2] マイケル・ジョーダン（1963-）は、NBA のシカゴ・ブルズを中心に活躍した元バスケットボール選手。15 年間の現役生活で得点王 10 回、年間最多得点 11 回、平均得点は 30.12 点で NBA 歴代 1 位である

Review the Key Expressions

各問、選択肢から適切な単語を選び、英文を完成させましょう。なお、余分な単語が１語ずつあります。

1. ハンターは藪の中の大きな動物をめがけて慎重に狙いを定め発砲した。

The hunter ( ) ( ) ( ) at the big ( ) in the ( ) and ( ).

fired took aim gave animal careful bush

2. この辺で地震が起きたので、その後遅い時間にひとりでとてもびくびくしていた。

I ( ) very ( ) being ( ) late in the day ( ) an earthquake ( ) ( ) in my area.

where alone had was because happened nervous

3. 東京五輪が延期になったと聞いた時、その選手は一言も話さなかった。ショックを受けた彼の表情がすべてを物語っていた。

When he ( ) that the Tokyo Olympics ( ) been ( ), the player didn't say ( ) ( ). His shocked expression ( ) it ( ).

said postponed heard had all word a complain

4. 大相撲の横綱白鵬は７場所［回］連続で優勝したことがある。

Yokozuna or grand champion of sumo ( ), Hakuho, ( ) ( ) the ( ) seven times ( ) ( ) ( ).

row in wrestling has championship after a won

● Discussion Questions

1. What are your hobbies? What sports or other things are you good at? Explain.

2. What is one situation you find frustrating or challenging? Explain.

UNIT 8 Boccia Boom Revitalizing Japanese Companies

企業に広がるボッチャ競技

パラリンピックの正式競技ボッチャが、一般の会社員の間でブームになっている。そのきっかけを作ったのが 2017 年に始まった企業対抗の競技会だ。試合の様子は、陸上版のカーリングにも見える。誰でも気軽に始められ、そのプレーの駆け引きのおもしろさが老若男女、健常者・障がい者を問わず、大きな魅力となっている。

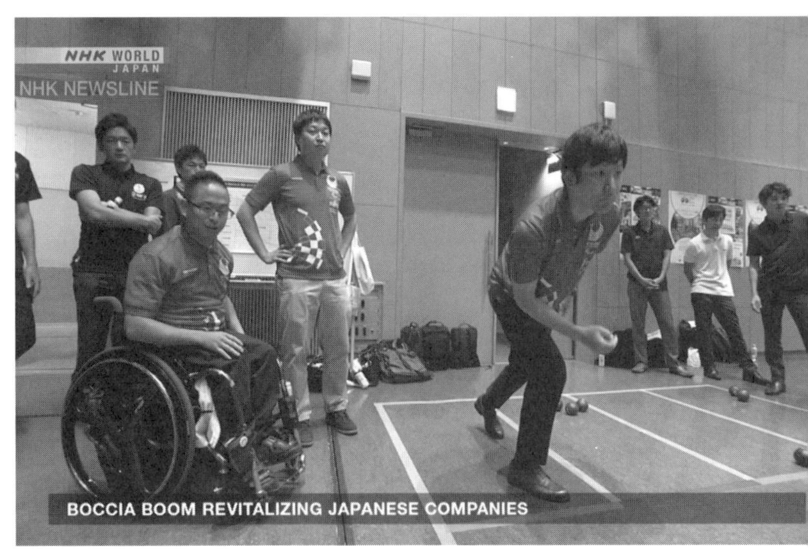

● Words & Phrases

CD 16

- ☐ to **revitalize**　～を活性化する
- ☐ **jack ball**　目標球、標的を示す（白い）ボール
- ☐ **the tables can turn**　形勢が逆転する〈特に、劣勢から優勢へ向かう場合〉
- ☐ to **be hooked on**　《口語》～に夢中になっている
- ☐ **face to face with**　～と向かい合って
- ☐ to **cheer up**　～を応援する、元気づける
- ☐ to **kick off**　～を始める
- ☐ **encouragement**　激励、励まし
- ☐ **fad**　一時的な流行

  Some two decades ago, owning an electronic toy called the tamagotchi was a *fad* among boys and girls.
  20 年ほど前、電子おもちゃの「たまごっち」（を持つこと）が男の子、女の子の間で流行った。
- ☐ **inclusive**　包括的な〈⇔ exclusive 排他的な〉

  Compared to the word chairman, *chairperson* is a more inclusive term since it includes both men and women. 「チェアマン」という言葉と比較して「チェアパーソン」は男女を含むので、より包括的な言葉だ。

Before You Watch

以下は、ボッチャに関するルール等の記述です。下の枠内から適切な単語を選び、空所に入れましょう。なお、２回使う単語もあります。

1. Boccia is played one-on-one, in pairs, or in ( ) of three players.

2. You and your opponent get six of the ( ) colored leather-like balls, either red or ( ).

3. A red team player throws the white ( ) ball, called the jack, onto the court and also throws the first red ball. Then the ( ) team player throws.

4. The goal of the game is to throw your ball as ( ) to the jack as possible.

5. The player whose ball is farther from the jack ( ) then throw until he/she puts a ball closer to the jack.

6. The player who puts the ball closest to the jack ( ) points for that end or inning.

7. The team with the ( ) scores at the end of the ( ) wins.

blue	close	earns	game	higher
must	same	target	teams	

Watch the News

First Viewing

ニュースを見て、内容と合っているものはT、違っているものはＦを選びましょう。

1. Over 70 companies participated in the championship round of the boccia event. [T / F]

2. This IT company voluntarily began a boccia event for disabled children. [T / F]

3. Yoshino's team won the league championship. [T / F]

Understand the News　Second Viewing

1 ニュースをもう一度見て、各問の空所に入る適切な選択肢をａ～ｃから選びましょう。

1. In boccia, the team will win if they ____.
  a. hit the white jack ball out of the court
  b. throw more balls nearer the jack ball
  c. hit many of the opposing team's balls out of the court

2. After this IT company's workers finish their work day, ____.
  a. they get together at a gym near their company
  b. they convert a regular meeting room into a boccia court
  c. they use their company's athletic facilities for practice

3. Shun Sato ____.
  a. won a medal at a Paralympic game
  b. is a boccia coach contracted with many companies
  c. is a boccia player employed by this IT company

2 次の各文を読み、ニュースの内容に合っているものを２つ選びましょう。

1. The jack ball can be either black or white.
2. Office de Boccia is the name of the office which organizes boccia games.
3. During the boccia event for disabled children, at least 40 volunteers helped.
4. This IT company has boccia members from their 20s to their 60s.
5. According to the narrator, many players are afraid that boccia may just be a fad.

3 CD の音声を聞いて、次ページ News Story の❶～❼の文中にある空所に適切な単語を書き入れましょう。音声は２回繰り返されます。 CD 17

● News Story

Narrator: After a long day at work, these people aren't going home or to the bar. ❶ They're ([1]) ([2]) ([3]) ([4]) ([5]) ([6]) one of Japan's hottest new trends. Welcome to Office de Boccia, an event that started two years ago. More than 70 companies are competing at this championship round. Players from both sides toss a ball toward a white **jack ball**. The team that throws more balls closest to the jack wins.

❶ ～に参加する準備をしている

Man: It's exciting because **the tables can turn** with just a single shot.

Woman: ❷ Anyone can enjoy the sport, and ([1]) ([2]) ([3]) ([4]) ([5]) ([6]).

❷ それは団結するという感覚を生み出す

Narrator: ❸ This IT company ([1]) ([2]) ([3]) ([4]) ([5]) ([6]) ([7]). System engineer Mayumi Yoshino has **been hooked on** boccia for more than four years. Yoshino spends most of her time **face to face with** the computer screen, but boccia has allowed her to interact with colleagues.

❸ ボッチャへの愛をとても真剣にとらえている

Coworker: She invited me, and we played boccia a couple of times, didn't we?

Mayumi Yoshino: We can also play with casual acquaintances who we have only known a short time, even with new employees and executives.

Narrator: They finish their work at 5:30, and now it's time to play. A meeting room is transformed into a boccia court. About 30 members, ranging in age from their 20s to 60s, are part of the club.

Shun Sato was hired last year, the first boccia athlete to be recruited by the company. In Japan, athletes are often employed by companies to work and compete in their sport with the support of the company. Sato is hoping to go to the Paralympics next year. ❹ Yoshino says Sato's influence and her experience playing boccia have changed ([1]) ([2]) ([3]) ([4]) ([5]) ([6]).

❹ 障がい者についての彼女の認識

Yoshino: We play together and share the same sports as teammates. ❺ I have realized *there's* * no obstacles between us, and I ([1]) ([2]) ([3]) ([4]) ([5]) ([6]).

❺ 他の人と同じように彼に接する

Shun Sato: My teammates here are like my second family for me. They always come to my games and **cheer** me **up**.

Narrator: Boccia has also helped the company to be more active in giving back to the community. They **kicked off** a boccia convention for children with disabilities. More than 40 employees volunteered at the event.

Iori Sakai ***(Chief manager, CAC Holdings Corporation):*** We would like to broaden our future corporate social responsibility activities. ❻ In addition to boccia, we are considering other activities ([1]) ([2]) ([3]) ([4]) ([5]) ([6]).

❻（それが）地域社会に貢献する

Narrator: Back at the league championship round, the company team is working together with Sato's **encouragement**.

Sato: Let's earn one point for sure.

Narrator: Yoshino threw some nice shots, but the team was defeated by a strong rival. ❼ In the end, though, the real win is ([1]) ([2]) ([3]) ([4]) ([5]).

❼ チームメイトの絆

The boccia boom is not just a temporary **fad**, and it is opening up the doors of Japanese companies to be more **inclusive** and interactive. Noriko Okada, NHK World.

Note ＊文法的には there are になる

Review the Key Expressions

各問、選択肢から適切な単語を選び、英文を完成させましょう。なお、余分な単語が１語ずつあります。

1. 彼はパチンコにはまっていて、金儲けしようとほとんど毎日やっている。

He is (　　　　　　) (　　　　　　) *pachinko* pinball games and (　　　　　　) them (　　　　　　) every day (　　　　　　) to (　　　　　　) money.

really　trying　make　almost　hooked　plays　on

2. その地震による死傷者の推定数は 1,000 人から 2,000 人までいろいろだ［〜の範囲にわたる］。

(　　　　　　) of the number of (　　　　　　) from the (　　　　　　) (　　　　　　) (　　　　　　) 1,000 (　　　　　　) 2,000.

varies　range　casualties　estimates　to　earthquake　from

3. ジョンが恋人と別れて落ち込んでいたので、私は精いっぱい彼を元気づけようとした。

John felt (　　　　　　) after he (　　　　　　) up (　　　　　　) his girlfriend, so I (　　　　　　) my best to (　　　　　　) him (　　　　　　).

cheer　broke　out　with　up　tried　depressed

4. 今日のミーティングを始めますが、まず最初に新しい企画について少し意見を述べたいと思います。

I'm (　　　　　　) to (　　　　　　) (　　　　　　) today's meeting (　　　　　　) a few (　　　　　　) about our new (　　　　　　).

project　off　going　with　out　remarks　kick

● Discussion Questions

1. If your company had a boccia club, would you be interested in joining it? Why or why not?

2. If you are a student, what club might you want to join and what activities?

UNIT 9 Rising Profile

人気のインスタ ——「東北女子」

東北地方の魅力を投稿しているインスタグラムのアカウントが話題である。このアカウント「東北女子」は、台湾人女性邱文心（きゅう ぶんしん）さんによって運営されているが、基本的には自分の行きたい場所を訪問し、周辺のレジャー情報とともに投稿する。桜や雪など季節に即した景色の紹介は評判も良く、フォロワー数もうなぎ登りである。

● Words & Phrases

CD 18

□ **exposure** （マスメディアなどへの）登場、取り上げられること
The young candidate for governor thought he could get more *exposure* on the television.
その若い知事候補者は、もっと頻繁にテレビに出ることができるかもしれないと考えた。

□ to **call out for** （ある行動など）を強く要求する

□ **dazzling** 鮮やかな、目もくらむような、見事な

□ **splendor** 豪華、輝き

□ **lotus** 《植物》ハス

□ **lush** （植物などが）青々とした

□ **scenery** 景色

□ **inbound** インバウンドの、本国行きの
The frequent natural disasters have been damaging Japan's *inbound* tourism.
頻発する自然災害が、外国人の訪日観光事業に損害を与えている。

□ **stunning** 《口語》目の覚めるような、驚くほど素晴らしい

□ **like** （インスタグラムの）「いいね！」

□ **kaleidoscope** 万華鏡

Before You Watch

以下は、旅行や買い物に関する表現です。空所に適切な文字を入れ、下のクロスワードを完成させましょう。

ACROSS

1. 自撮りする　take a (**s** _ _ _ _ _)
2.《レストランで》３人席でお願いします。(**T** _ _ _ _) for three, please.
3. 観光バス　(**s** _ _ _ _ _ _ _ _ _ _) bus　**4.** お土産　(**s** _ _ _ _ _ _ _)

DOWN

1. 旅行代理店　travel (_ _ _ _ _ _)
5.《ファストフード店で》店内で、それともお持ち帰りですか。For here or to (_ _)?
6. 旅行日程　(**i** _ _ _ _ _ _ _ _)　**8.** 旅行する　go (_ _) a trip
7. 出張　(**b** _ _ _ _ _ _ _) trip　**9.** どうぞ楽しい空の旅を。Have a nice (_ _ _ _ _ _).

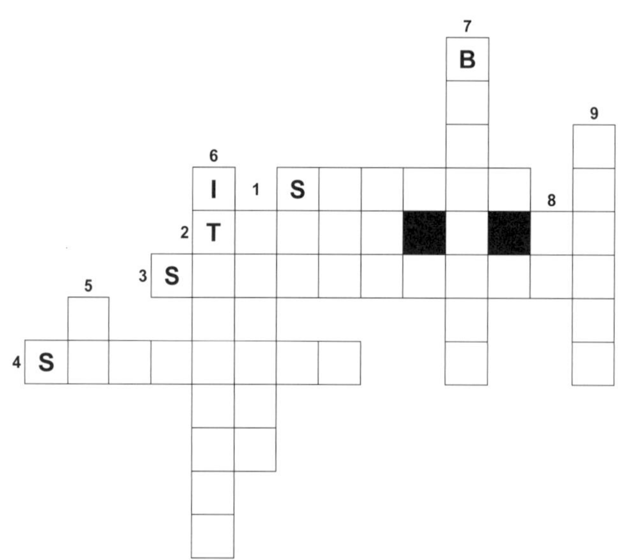

Watch the News　First Viewing

ニュースを見て、内容と合っているものはT、違っているものはFを選びましょう。

1. The Tohoku region has recently been a popular destination for foreign visitors.　[T / F]
2. Chiu Wen-hsin is a Taiwanese who was born in Japan.　[T / F]
3. Shi visited Japan on a free trip thanks to Chiu's company.　[T / F]

Understand the News

Second Viewing

1 ニュースをもう一度見て、各問の空所に入る適切な選択肢をa～cから選びましょう。

1. Chiu's Instagram is very popular and she ____.

a. is going to open an English version for people all over the world

b. is also planning to post pictures of other Japanese regions

c. has over 5,000 followers, many of whom are Taiwanese

2. Chiu mainly targets ____.

a. young female Taiwanese

b. Japanese people who don't live in the Tohoku region

c. anyone who wants to share her adventures in Taiwan

3. Shi feels that the real Akiu Otaki Waterfall ____.

a. would look the best in fall amid the colored leaves

b. looks more powerful than in the pictures

c. appears smaller than she imagined from Chiu's Instagram

2 以下の各情報を、ニュースに出てきた順序に並べましょう。

1. Akiu Otaki Waterfall is popular and the Instagram picture of it gets many *likes*.

2. A snapshot of souvenir candy is shown on Chiu's Instagram.

3. Shi says that she was impressed by a lot of the pictures on Chiu's Instagram.

4. Chiu says that she likes the peaceful atmosphere of the Tohoku region.

3 CDの音声を聞いて、次ページNews Storyの❶～❼の文中にある空所に適切な単語を書き入れましょう。音声は2回繰り返されます。 CD 19

● News Story

Anchor: Japan has been attracting more tourists every year, but in 2017 only one percent went to the Tohoku region. This next story looks at a young woman from Taiwan who's working to give the northeast more **exposure**, using the power of social media.

Narrator: An island bridge **calls out for** you to cross, and a souvenir candy too **dazzling** to eat. Snapshots of Tohoku in all its **splendor**. They appear on an Instagram page, all captioned in Chinese.

(*From Instagram page*) "Enjoy Kurihara's blooming **lotus** flowers from a boat."

The page is run by an Instagram user called Tohoku Girl. Chiu Wen-hsin started the page. ❶ Originally from Taiwan, (　　　[1]) (　　　[2]) (　　　[3]) (　　　[4]) (　　　[5]) (　　　[6]) (　　　[7]) in Sendai City, Miyagi Prefecture.

Chiu: Tohoku's **lush**, natural environment is beautiful. ❷ (　　　[1]) (　　　[2]) (　　　[3]) (　　　[4]) (　　　[5]) in the region, even in the cities. ❸ (　　　[1]) (　　　[2]) (　　　[3]) (　　　[4]) (　　　[5]) (　　　[6]) is its relaxed atmosphere.

Narrator: Chiu says there's always something new to discover in her new home. And she's using Instagram to share her passion. She currently has around 5,200 followers, many from Taiwan.

(*Message from a follower*) "All of the food and sights posted on this page look fantastic. I would love to go there and experience them for myself."

Her user name, Tohoku Girl, hints at her target audience, young women. She thinks many would enjoy the relaxed feel of the Tohoku region.

❶ 今彼女は広告代理店で働いている

❷ どこでもとても居心地が良いと感じる

❸ その地域で私が気に入っていること

Chiu: Whether it's a beautiful Japanese dish or some **scenery** that looks exotic to a Taiwanese eye, I hope to share snapshots that capture the flavor of a place at a specific moment.

Narrator: An **inbound** flight from Taiwan. Shi Wei-ling is one of Chiu's followers.

Shi: It's my first visit and I'm very excited. ❹ I'm ([1]) ([2]) ([3]) ([4]) ([5]) ([6]) ([7]). The pictures on Instagram were **stunning**!

❹ 観光地に行くのを楽しみにしている

Narrator: ❺ Shi won a free trip to Japan offered by Chiu's advertising agency, which means she has the ([1]) ([2]) ([3]) ([4]) ([5]) ([6]). Chiu starts with a natural wonder.

❺ 彼女を案内するのに完璧なガイド

Chiu: (*Looking at a waterfall*) This is amazing!

Shi: Is it usually like this?

Chiu: No, it's not always like this.

Narrator: The Akiu Otaki Waterfall picture always gets plenty of ***likes*** on Chiu's page, but Shi finds the real waterfall looks even more dynamic, thanks to recent heavy rain. Next up, a **kaleidoscope** museum for dynamic vision of a different kind.

Shi: I think the natural environment was richer than I imagined from the pictures. I feel very refreshed. I really enjoyed it.

Chiu: ❻ I'm really happy that ([1]) ([2]) ([3]) ([4]) ([5]) ([6]) and was finally able to visit the actual sites. I hope to keep posting to my Instagram page and serve as a bridge between Taiwan and Tohoku, Japan.

❻ 誰かが私の写真に刺激を受けた

Narrator: ❼ Tohoku ([1]) ([2]) ([3]) ([4]) ([5]). Chiu's social networking is bringing her adopted home into the spotlight, one post at a time.

❼ 外国人には比較的知られないままである

Review the Key Expressions

各問、選択肢から適切な単語を選び、英文を完成させましょう。なお、余分な単語が１語ずつあります。

1. その夫婦が離婚する前は、いつも喜びや悲しみを共にしていた。

( ) the ( ) ( ), they ( ) always ( ) their joys and ( ).

shared sorrows before got couple had divorced

2. 脚を組んで［交差させて］就職の面接を受けるのは、日本人の目には不適切に映る。

( ) with your legs ( ) during a ( ) ( ) looks ( ) to a Japanese ( ).

proper eye sitting job crossed inappropriate interview

3. 雨模様の日が長く続いた後で（久しぶりに）公園を散歩したら、とてもリフレッシュできた［爽快感があった］。

When I ( ) a ( ) around the park after ( ) many ( ) days, I really ( ) ( ).

rainy felt relied walk refreshed so took

4. バラク・オバマは大統領在任期間８年間に、黒人と白人の架け橋［として］の役目を果たした。

Barack Obama ( ) ( ) a ( ) ( ) Blacks and Whites ( ) his eight years as ( ).

President during between served bridge as role

● Discussion Questions

1. If you take foreign visitors around Japan, where will you go? Why?

2. What are your favorite apps and why do you like them?

UNIT 10 All Blacks Cause City to Rethink Ink

ラグビーがつなぐリスペクト

文化や風習の違いがしばしば誤解を生みだすこともある。2019年に行われたラグビーワールドカップ日本大会では、ニュージーランド代表オールブラックスと別府市民の交流行事が開催された。訪問した選手やファンの「入れ墨」が日本の温泉でどのように扱われるべきかが論議になったが、お互いへの理解と尊重という姿勢で解決を図った。

● Words & Phrases

CD 20

- ☐ **ink**　墨〈ここでは入れ墨を指す。reth<u>ink</u> と韻を踏む〉
- ☐ **splash**　《口語》一時的な大騒ぎ
  He made a *splash* with his new comic book series.
  彼は新しいマンガのシリーズで評判を得た。
- ☐ **stereotype**　（社会集団の）固定観念
- ☐ **skin-deep**　うわべだけの
- ☐ **enthusiastic**　熱狂的な
- ☐ **indigenous**　固有の、原産の
  Blueberries are *indigenous* to America.
  ブルーベリーはアメリカ原産である。
- ☐ **tats**　《口語》入れ墨〈tatts というつづりもある〉
- ☐ **self-conscious**　自意識の強い
- ☐ **proprietor**　所有者
- ☐ **supercharged**　《口語》より強力な
- ☐ **indelible**　消せない

Before You Watch

以下は、いろいろな球技に関する説明です。下の枠内から適切な語句を選び、空所に入れましょう。ただし、余分な語句もあります。

Sports	Origin (where)	First Played (when)	Rules, etc.
1. ( )	England	first half of the 19th century	The ball can be passed laterally or backwards, but ( ) passing is not allowed.
2. ( )	USA	1891	After a foul play, the player fouled or another player of the team is qualified to make one or more ( ) throws.
3. ( )	USA	1895	For each rally a team may touch the ball up to ( ) times, but the same players are not allowed to touch the ball consecutively.
4. ( ) 〈modern version〉	USA	19th century	Unlike the playing area of most other sports, playing fields vary significantly in ( ) and shape.
5. ( )	England	1880s	During ( ), the ball must be tossed at least 16 cm into the air.
6. ( ) 〈modern version〉	England	Between 1859 and 65	In a game, scores from zero to three points are respectively called as ( ), 15, 30 and 40.
7. ( )	England	Mid-19th century	Except for the goalkeepers, players are not allowed to touch the ball with hands or ( ).

arms	baseball	basketball	forward	free	golf	lacrosse	love
rugby	service	size	soccer	table tennis	tennis	three	volleyball

Watch the News

First Viewing

ニュースを見て、内容と合っているものはT、違っているものはFを選びましょう。

1. The All Blacks chose Beppu City as the World Cup venue. [T / F]

2. In Japan, tattoos are often associated with gangsters. [T / F]

3. All the Beppu spa inns decided to accept foreign visitors with tattoos. [T / F]

Understand the News　Second Viewing

1 ニュースをもう一度見て、各問の空所に入る適切な選択肢を a ～ c から選びましょう。

1. Tattoos ____.

a. remind New Zealanders of gangsters

b. are parts of the traditional culture of New Zealand

c. were introduced to New Zealand by the younger generation

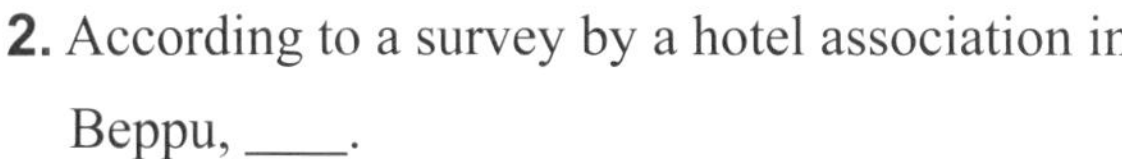

2. According to a survey by a hotel association in Beppu, ____.

a. more than half of the guests don't accept tattoos

b. two-thirds of the guests are not against tattoos

c. one-third of the customers say tattoos are cool

3. The All Black players tried their best ____.

a. not to use public baths while other tourists were around

b. to take sand baths instead of regular, hot water baths

c. not to show their tattoos in public

2 以下はニュースの概要です。空所に適切な単語を書き入れましょう。語頭の文字(群)は与えてあります。

New Zealand's (**n** [1]) rugby team is training in Beppu, a spa town, for the World Cup being held in Japan. The team is called the All Blacks, and its members love (**re** [2]) in *onsens*. The only problem is that they have tattoos, which are a respected part of (**ind** [3]) culture in New Zealand. But in Japan, tattoos are often associated with (**ga** [4]). Nevertheless, many Beppu facilities are understanding and warmly (**we** [5]) foreign customers with tattoos. Also, those players respect Japanese culture and try not to expose their tattoos. They even promote Beppu's spas by taking (**s** [6]) baths.

3 CD の音声を聞いて、次ページ News Story の❶～❼の文中にある空所に適切な単語を書き入れましょう。音声は 2 回繰り返されます。 CD 21

● News Story

Anchor: Next, New Zealand's national rugby team makes a **splash** wherever it goes. ❶ For the World Cup, now underway here in Japan, the All Blacks trained in a part of Japan ([1]) ([2]) ([3]) ([4]) ([5]) ([6]). The team quickly got accustomed to the water, and people in the community learned to look beyond **stereotypes** that are only **skin-deep**.

❶ 温泉で有名な（場所）

Narrator: ❷ The All Blacks ([1]) ([2]) ([3]) ([4]) ([5]) ([6]) Beppu. The team chose the city as a training site.

❷ ～で温かい歓迎を受けた

Kieran Read (Captain of the All Blacks): It's great for us to be here and *hopeful**1... We can't wait. We are looking forward to a relaxing *onsen*.

Woman: (*She talks about the players.*) This might be my only chance to see them.

Boy: Great! They're huge!

Narrator: ❸ The city was **enthusiastic**, but ([1]) ([2]) ([3]) ([4]) ([5]) ([6]) all those tattoos. In Japanese *onsen*, tattoos are often taboo because of their association with gangsters. But tattoos are part of New Zealand's **indigenous** culture.

❸ その市は～についてどうするか悩んでいた

A Beppu hotel association conducted a survey of guests. A third of them were against tolerating the **tats**. On the other hand, many overseas fans were planning to stay in Beppu during the tournament.

Rugby fan: We can't come to Beppu and not have an*2 *onsen*.

Narrator: ❹ (　　　　[1]) (　　　　[2]) (　　　　[3]) (　　　　[4]). About 100 facilities allowed customers with tattoos to enter, and the tourist information center spread the word.

> ❹ 妥協点が見つかった

Tomomi Hatayama (Tourist Information Center): ❺ (　　　　[1]) (　　　　[2]) (　　　　[3]) (　　　　[4]) (　　　　[5]) they can't enter an *onsen* if they have tattoos, but in Beppu, we say it's okay.

> ❺ 海外からの観光客には〜と考える人もいる

Narrator: Some of the facilities that accepted tattoos offered additional services. People who might feel **self-conscious** could rent private outdoor baths.

Maya Honda (Proprietor, hot spring inn): The hot spring industry can compromise a bit so that international visitors are able to enjoy Japanese *onsen* and take home good memories.

Narrator: ❻ Residents found the New Zealand players (　　　　[1]) (　　　　[2]) (　　　　[3]) (　　　　[4]) (　　　　[5]) (　　　　[6]) (　　　　[7]).

> ❻ 溶け込むように精いっぱい努力していた

Aaron Smith (All Blacks): And it's okay. This is ah... We're in Japan. We are going to embrace their way, their culture.

Narrator: They wore clothing to the public baths and were careful not to expose their tattoos.

❼ The team (　　　　[1]) (　　　　[2]) (　　　　[3]) (　　　　[4]) (　　　　[5]) of the players enjoying sand baths, giving the city some **supercharged**, international PR.

> ❼ ビデオをウェブサイトに上げた

In the end, the tattoos hardly caused a stir in Beppu. But through their thoughtfulness, the All Blacks *left an* ***indelible*** *mark**[3].

Notes

*[1] 発音があまり明瞭ではない

*[2] ここは a のように聞こえるが、文法的には an が正しい

*[3] 入れ墨の話だけに「選手たちはずっと消せない、思い出に残る印を残した」とまとめている

Review the Key Expressions

各問、選択肢から適切な単語を選び、英文を完成させましょう。なお、余分な単語が１語ずつあります。

1. ズームを使ったオンライン会議に慣れるとはとても思えない。

I ( ) think ( ) ever ( ) ( ) to ( ) online ( ) on Zoom.

accustomed don't I'll meetings having get hold

2. それは不幸な出来事だったが、その一方で、私たちは自分たちの間違いから学んだ。

It ( ) an ( ) accident, but ( ) the ( ) ( ), we learned from our ( ).

other unnecessary on was unfortunate mistakes hand

3. ジェイミー・オリバーは、健康に気を付けて食事をし、体調を維持しておく重要性について広く知らせた。

Jamie Oliver ( ) ( ) ( ) about the ( ) of ( ) eating and ( ) fit.

accepted staying spread word importance the healthy

4. そのウイルスが発生してから客は一人も来なくなった。（そして）最後にそのレストランは廃業に追い込まれた。

( ) a ( ) customer came after the ( ) of the virus. In the ( ), the restaurant ( ) out of ( ).

end single business many outbreak went not

● Discussion Questions

1. What do you think of tattoos? Do you have different impressions of Japanese people with tattoos than of foreign visitors with them?

2. Soaking in *onsens* is a part of Japanese culture. What Japanese cultural activities do you enjoy or are you proud of?

UNIT 11 Man-made Threat to Japanese Deer

鹿を守れ！プラごみの脅威

天然記念物である「奈良の鹿」がポリ袋を食べて死ぬ事故が多発している。鹿が袋に残った食品の臭いをかいで食べ、それが胃に詰まった結果だという。愛護団体は、鹿を守るには観光客が鹿せんべいだけを与え、ごみをいっさい捨てないことが重要だと訴える。今後は、食べても害がない袋の普及も期待されている。

NHK WORLD JAPAN
PLASTIC WASTE IS THREATENING JAPAN'S DEER

● Words & Phrases

CD 22

- □ **carcass** （獣の）死体
- □ to **snatch** ひったくる
- □ to **forage** 〈食糧を〉捜し回る
- □ **bin** 蓋つきの大箱
- □ **surge** 急激な増加
  The venture firm is expecting a 50% *surge* in sales this year.
  そのベンチャー企業は、今年 50%の売り上げ増を期待している。
- □ **littering** 〈ごみ・くずなどを〉散らかすこと
- □ to **pitch in** 協力する
- □ to **crowdfund** クラウドファンディングする〈協賛者から資金調達をすること〉
- □ to **fan out** （扇形に）広がる
- □ **human wave technique** 人海戦術
- □ to **eye** ～を（じろじろ）見る
  The kids *eyed* the tourist with curiosity.
  子供たちは好奇心からその旅行者をじろじろ見つめた。
- □ **close call** 《口語》危うく逃れること、危機一髪
- □ to **ingest** ～を摂取する
- □ to **curb** ～を抑制する、抑える

Before You Watch

以下は、天然記念物や世界遺産などに関する記述です。下の枠内から適切な語彙を選び、空所に入れましょう。なお、語頭が大文字になる場合もあります。

1. 世界遺産には厳島神社や古都奈良の文化財が含まれる。
World Heritage Sites include Itsukushima Shinto Shrine and the Historic Monuments of ( ) Nara.

2. 世界遺産のリストに、知床半島が自然遺産として2005年に加えられた。
The Shiretoko ( ) was added to the World Heritage List as a Natural Heritage Site in 2005.

3. 富士山は自然遺産ではなく文化遺産として2013年に登録された。
Mt Fuji was registered not as a Natural Heritage Site but as a ( ) Heritage Site in 2013.

4. 長野県の松本城は国宝に指定されている。
Matsumoto Castle in Nagano Prefecture is listed as a ( ) Treasure of Japan.

5. 国の特別天然記念物のコウノトリが先月ふ化した。
Baby ( ), special ( ) treasures of Japan, hatched last month.

6. 歌舞伎や能は無形文化財と呼ばれる。
Kabuki and Noh plays are called ( ) cultural properties.

7. アメリカバイソンとラッコは絶滅危惧種の例である。
American bison and sea ( ) are examples of ( ) species.

ancient	cultural	endangered	intangible	
national	natural	otters	peninsula	storks

Watch the News　First Viewing

ニュースを見て、内容と合っているものはT、違っているものはFを選びましょう。

1. This mass of stuff is full of plastics and was found in a dead deer's stomach. [T / F]
2. Tourists are attracted to anything with the scent of food in the park. [T / F]
3. It's important to keep in mind that we should decrease the amount of garbage. [T / F]

Understand the News　Second Viewing

1 ニュースをもう一度見て、各問の空所に入る適切な選択肢を a～c から選びましょう。

1. Visitors ____.

a. scatter and don't use the waste bins correctly

b. can't find any waste baskets in Nara Park

c. carry reusable bags and don't need public garbage bins

2. Local people near the park ____.

a. want to sell more crackers for deer online

b. sell reusable bags to prevent people from discarding disposable kinds

c. found out that plastics are digested in deer's stomachs

3. Volunteers in Nara Park ____.

a. tried to remove all the pieces of plastic waste from the area

b. get plastic bags back from the deer in a relatively simple manner

c. can't warn tourists because they might get angry and leave the park

2 右の文字列を並べ替えて単語を作り、各文の空所に入れて意味がとおるようにしましょう。語頭の文字が与えてあるものもあります。

1. Local people decided to take (**a**) to protect the deer in Nara Park. [ntico]

2. You see the same sign all over the park, "No (**L**)." [gettinir]

3. This store near the park is selling reusable bags made of ( ). [ntootc]

4. The deer almost stole plastic bags from the (**t**). 〈複数形〉 [sitsour]

3 CD の音声を聞いて、次ページ News Story の❶～❼の文中にある空所に適切な単語を書き入れましょう。音声は２回繰り返されます。 CD 23

● News Story

Narrator: This tangled mass weighing over four kilograms was removed from a dead deer's stomach. After inspecting it, an all-too-familiar item emerged.

Worker: It's a bag.

Narrator: ❶ Most likely ([1]) ([2]) ([3]) ([4]) ([5]) ([6]) ([7]), almost all of it hardened plastic waste. ❷ Unable to digest it, ([1]) ([2]) ([3]) ([4]) ([5]).

❶ 買い物袋や飴の包み紙

❷ 鹿は倒れて死んだ

Since March, similar masses have been found in five deer **carcasses**, raising concern that many of the park's mascots will die from consuming plastic.

Seeing deer in the park feeding on plastic is unfortunately all too common. They're attracted to anything with the scent of food. While tourists feed them crackers, they **snatch** away plastic bags. ❸ They also **forage** on the garbage ([1]) ([2]) ([3]) ([4]) ([5]).

❸ 後に残された（ごみ）

There are no waste **bins** in the park to prevent deer from getting into them. But with the recent **surge** in tourism, **littering** is on the rise.

Locals are taking action themselves to protect the deer. This store near Nara Park is **pitching in** by selling reusable cotton bags.

❹ A local company **crowdfunded** resources to produce the deer motif bags ([1]) ([2]) ([3]) ([4]) ([5]).

❹ 会社がオンラインでも販売するもの

Kanako Adachi** **(Designer, Shintosha director): Ideally, people would refuse plastic bags. I hope they will put items they purchase, such as drinks, in a reusable bag before going to the park.

Narrator: Volunteers **fan out** over the entire park using the **human wave technique**. They track deer habitats, such as their drinking areas, and remove individual pieces of plastic waste.

Volunteer 1: The deer is going for his bag.

Narrator: This volunteer warns a tourist.

Volunteer 1: He's **eyeing** it.

Narrator: When necessary, they take direct measures. (*The volunteer takes away a bag from a deer.*)

Reporter: (*He looks at the bag.*) It's chewed on.

Volunteer 2: But he hasn't swallowed it. ❺ ([1]) ([2]) ([3]) ([4]) ([5]).

❺ そうすることを何とか防止できた

Reporter: Do you have many **close calls** a day?

Volunteer 2: Yes, we do. ❻ ([1]) ([2]) ([3]) ([4]) ([5]) ([6]) a tourist, I don't think the person will get it back.

❻ もし鹿が～(から) の何かをつかんだら

Rie Maruko (Veterinarian): It's like the deer's stomachs are becoming garbage cans. Many are at risk of dying by **ingesting** plastics. So, it's vital that humans work to reduce the amount of garbage we produce.

Narrator: The co-existence of deer and humans is now threatened. ❼ It's up to us to **curb** our careless waste if we want to ([1]) ([2]) ([3]) ([4]) ([5]) ([6]).

❼ 両者の利益になる関係を維持する

Review the Key Expressions

各問、選択肢から適切な単語を選び、英文を完成させましょう。なお、余分な単語が1語ずつあります。

1. バンクシーが誰なのか知る人はいないが、彼の絵画や素描は値上がりしている。

( ) knows ( ) Banksy is, but the ( ) of his paintings and ( ) is ( ) the ( ).

who rise drawings price on ride nobody

2. その社員たちが一時解雇されるとすぐに、組合側は労働者を守る行動をとる決断をした。

As ( ) as the ( ) were ( ) ( ), the union decided to take ( ) to ( ) the workers.

defend action employees off soon laid while

3. 多くのプロレスラーは何度も危機一髪の経験をするが、リングで重症を負う者もいる。

Many pro wrestlers have a ( ) of ( ) ( ), and ( ) are seriously ( ) in the ( ).

some calls ring close link injured lot

4. 前に長い列ができているけれど、並び続けるかその乗り物をあきらめるかは君次第だ。

There is a long line in ( ) ( ) us. It's ( ) ( ) you ( ) we ( ) in line or ( ) the ride.

skip front whether of down up stay to

● Discussion Questions

1. What would you suggest people do to prevent deer in Nara Park from eating plastic?

2. Every store is now charging for disposable plastic bags. Do you think it's a good idea? Why or why not?

UNIT 12 Home Appliance Maker Leads Comeback

家電メーカー
—— 海外の巻き返しを図れ！

日本製の家電は高品質だが、売上ベースの世界シェアでは名前が上位にあまり出てこない。そんな中、家電メーカーで生活用品にも携わるアイリスオーヤマが、海外での製品販売を強化している。数ある種類の製品の中で今回開発したのが静電モップを搭載した極細軽量スティッククリーナー。その開発の苦心をかいま見る。

● Words & Phrases

CD 24

- □ **home appliance**　家電
- □ to **overestimate**　～を過大評価する
- □ to **prioritize**　～を優先させる
- □ **edge**　《略式》優位
- □ **Chinese dumpling**　餃子
- □ **suction**　吸引（力）
- □ **endorsement**　支持、是認
- □ **gravel**　砂利
- □ to **hold down**　〈価格など〉を抑える
  The rate of inflation must be *held down*.
  インフレの割合［程度］を抑えておかなければならない。
- □ **up-and-coming**　有望な、将来性のある
  The new Hokkaido governor seems to be an *up-and-coming* government leader.
  北海道の新知事は有望な政治リーダーのようだ。

Before You Watch

以下は、家電に関する語彙です。１～９の空所に当てはまる英語を下のアルファベット表から見つけ、線で囲みましょう。囲み方は縦、横、斜めのいずれも可能です。

例：炊飯器　(rice) cooker

・電気掃除機　(　　　[1]) cleaner
・エアコン　air conditioner
・冷蔵庫　(　　　[2])
・ミシン　sewing machine
・電子レンジ　(　　　[3]) oven
・オーブントースター　(　　　[4]) oven
・洗濯機　(　　　[5]) machine
・スマホ　smartphone
・圧力鍋　(　　　[6]) cooker
・ガスコンロ　(　　　[7])
・加湿器　humidifier
・扇風機　electric (　　　[8])
・ノートパソコン　(　　　[9]) computer

	1	2	3	4	5	6	7	8	9	10	11	12	13	14	15	16
a	V	R	R	E	F	R	I	G	E	R	A	T	O	R	M	**R**
b	A	A	C	E	L	L	S	M	I	C	R	O	V	E	I	**I**
c	M	I	C	R	O	W	A	V	E	E	P	A	E	F	C	**C**
d	I	Z	H	U	M	E	L	P	R	E	S	S	U	R	E	**E**
e	N	J	G	S	U	W	O	N	T	N	O	T	G	I	M	F
f	G	E	A	M	O	M	N	S	T	O	V	E	U	G	I	A
g	W	A	S	H	I	N	G	S	A	W	P	R	L	O	T	N

Watch the News　First Viewing

ニュースを見て、内容と合っているものはＴ、違っているものはＦを選びましょう。

1. Japan has always had a reputation for low-priced, quality goods. [T / F]
2. IRIS Ohyama made an entry into the home appliance market a decade or so ago. [T / F]
3. In most Taiwanese homes, people take their shoes off when they enter. [T / F]

Understand the News　　Second Viewing

1 ニュースをもう一度見て、各問の空所に入る適切な選択肢を a ～ c から選びましょう。

1. Recently ____ electronic goods have been more popular than Japanese products.
- **a.** American and European
- **b.** Taiwanese and Malaysian
- **c.** Chinese and South Korean

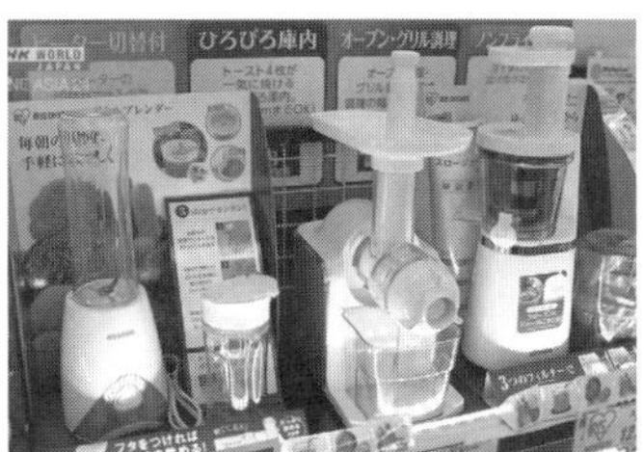

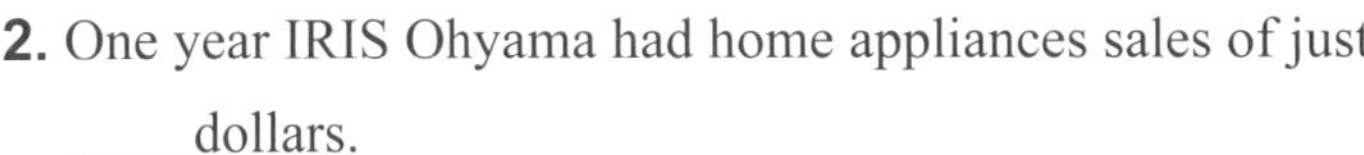

2. One year IRIS Ohyama had home appliances sales of just ____ dollars.
- **a.** about 750 thousand
- **b.** around 75 million
- **c.** under one billion

3. The appliance maker plans to start selling ____.
- **a.** vacuum cleaners with mops
- **b.** microwave ovens with grill functions
- **c.** rice cookers which cook different types of rice

2 以下はニュースの概要です。空所に適切な単語を書き入れましょう。語頭の文字(群)は与えてあります。

Leading Japanese manufacturers of electronic goods are not very successful overseas, although they have (**b** [1]) power. Their products are very expensive. IRIS Ohyama is relatively new and has made big advances into the housewares market. The company is planning to sell (**li** [2]) vacuum cleaners in (**T** [3]) soon. In the process of testing their product, they found out that their cleaners needed more (**su** [4]) power, and decided to use more powerful (**m** [5]). The company also (**h** [6]) down the cost of their products. Such newly produced Japanese electronics can make a comeback abroad.

3 CD の音声を聞いて、次ページ News Story の❶～❼の文中にある空所に適切な単語を書き入れましょう。音声は 2 回繰り返されます。　CD 25

● News Story

Anchor: The "Made in Japan" mark used to mean quality electronic goods, but leading Japanese makers **overestimated** their brand power and **prioritized** technology over price, allowing competitors from China, Taiwan or South Korea to gain an **edge** over the past decade. ❶ Yet, one household commodity maker (　　　[1]) (　　　[2]) (　　　[3]) (　　　[4]) (　　　[5]). NHK World's *Misaki*[*1] Fujii reports.

❶ 海外での成功を求めている

Narrator: IRIS Ohyama is based in Sendai, one of the largest cities in the Tohoku region. ❷ (　　　[1]) (　　　[2]) (　　　[3]) (　　　[4]) (　　　[5]) (　　　[6]) in the housewares market by meeting the needs of Japanese consumers precisely.

❷ その会社は急成長を遂げた

About ten years ago IRIS Ohyama enters the home appliance market. It's recruiting engineers who have left major electronics makers and (is) developing original products.[*2]

Man: I was just looking for a job when the company set up the research center. The timing was right, and I got the job. ❸ I want to make use of my experience and (　　　[1]) (　　　[2]) (　　　[3]) (　　　[4]) (　　　[5]).

❸ よく売れる商品を開発する

Narrator: Among its products is this microwave oven, which can also be used to grill **Chinese dumplings** or fish. This rice cooker can adjust to cook different types of rice. Last year, IRIS Ohyama posted home appliances sales of about 750 million dollars, proof that the firm has become one of Japan's top electronics makers.

The company is planning to release this lightweight vacuum cleaner in Taiwan this fall. It's designed to be able to sweep the floor with the attached mop and then vacuum up the dust stuck to the mop. ❹ The product was (　　　[1]) (　　　[2]) (　　　[3]) (　　　[4]) (　　　[5]) (　　　[6]) Taiwan.

❹ ～をよく知っている中国の社員によって評価が行われて

Shirley Sha ***(Senior Manager, Dalian IRIS Ohyama Development):*** It is light but the **suction** is weak.

Narrator: Why didn't it get their **endorsement**? ❺ In Japan, people (　　　[1]) (　　　[2]) (　　　[3]) (　　　[4]) (　　　[5]) (　　　[6]), whereas many Taiwanese keep their shoes on in their houses. ❻ Vacuum cleaners have to (　　　[1]) (　　　[2]) (　　　[3]) (　　　[4]) (　　　[5]) (　　　[6]) or **gravel** brought into the room.

❺ 家の中では靴を脱ぐ

❻ 泥を吸いこむくらい吸引力が強い

To increase its suction power, the engineers adopted a more powerful motor which was also more expensive. The company **held down** the cost by self-manufacturing the other parts.

Yoshiki Mori ***(Assistant Manager, IRIS Ohyama):*** The most important point is to resolve inconveniences faced by our customers. ❼ We (　　　[1]) (　　　[2]) (　　　[3]) (　　　[4]) (　　　[5]) (　　　[6]) and develop better products.

❼ 海外からの反応を調べる

Narrator: Will Japanese electronics be able to stage a comeback? One **up-and-coming** maker feels up to the challenge and aims to start the revival in Taiwan. Misaki Fujii, NHK World.

Notes

*[1] 名前の発音に誤りがある

*[2] この3行に関しては時制を現在に統一している。おそらく表現を生き生きさせるためと考えられる

Review the Key Expressions

各問、選択肢から適切な単語を選び、英文を完成させましょう。なお、余分な単語が１語ずつあります。

1. そのお寺の施設は、海外からの訪問客のニーズに合うように改修された。

The (　　　　　) (　　　　　) were (　　　　　) to (　　　　　) the (　　　　　) of visitors from (　　　　　).

remodeled　reformed　needs　temple　facilities　overseas　meet

2. その慈善団体は、寄付された家具やオフィスの備品を新しい支部で十分に利用した。

The charity organization (　　　　　) full (　　　　　) (　　　　　) the (　　　　　) furniture and office (　　　　　) at its new (　　　　　).

donated　made　branch　of　took　equipment　use

3. ほとんどの人々は、そのアフリカの国の習慣やならわしをよく知ら［〜に精通してい］ない。

(　　　　　) people (　　　　　) (　　　　　) very (　　　　　) (　　　　　) the (　　　　　) and practices of African countries.

customs　familiar　almost　not　most　with　are

4. 建物に入るときに靴を脱がなかったので、そのお寺では一時的に海外からの訪問客の受け入れをやめた。

The temple (　　　　　) stopped (　　　　　) visitors from (　　　　　) because they didn't (　　　　　) (　　　　　) their shoes before (　　　　　) the building.

entering　accepting　take　temporarily　put　off　overseas

● Discussion Questions

1. What is your favorite electronic product which you could not live without? Explain why.

2. Name one Japanese custom that you are proud of. Explain.

UNIT 13

Hospitals Breaking Down Language Barrier

広がる医療通訳

国際的行事・活動に重要な役割を担い、観光立国の実現を目指す日本。外国からの観光客招致に伴って避けて通れないのが言語の壁である。単に観光目的なら冊子での対応は不可能ではないだろうが、急を要するもの、特に緊急医療処置の際に病院ではどのように対処しているだろうか。現状をリポートする。

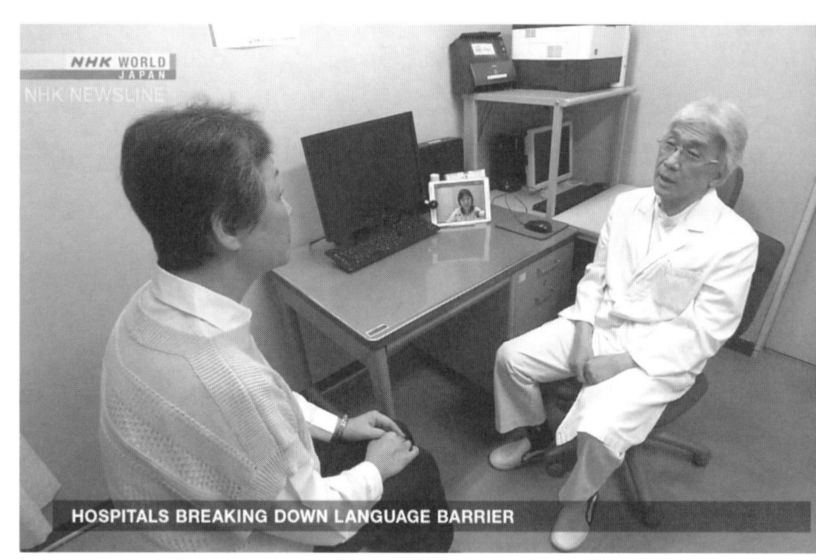

● Words & Phrases

CD 26

- □ **influx**　流入
- □ **dedicated to**　～専用の
- □ **interpreter**　通訳
- □ **peace of mind**　心の平安、平穏
  Having a good job and money in the bank gives most people some *peace of mind*.
  良い仕事に就き、銀行に貯金があればほとんどの人は心の平安が得られる。
- □ **technical word**　専門用語
- □ **on hand**　待機して、利用可能で
  There was a doctor *on hand* at the rugby game in case anyone got injured.
  けが人が出た場合に備えて、そのラグビーの試合では医者が待機していた。
- □ **tack**　対策、やり方
- □ **city authorities**　市当局
- □ **diagnosis**　診断
- □ **on site**　現場に
- □ **World Expo (= World Exposition)**　万国博覧会

Before You Watch

以下は、体の不調に関する表現です。下の枠内から適切な語彙を選び、空所に入れましょう。なお、余分な単語もあります。

1. おなかがとても痛い。 My (　　　　) really hurts.
2. 熱とひどい頭痛がある。 I have a (　　　　) and a bad (　　　　).
3. インフルエンザに罹ったかもしれない。 I may have the (　　　　).
4. めまいがする。 I'm (　　　　).
5. 寒気がして咳がひどい。 I have (　　　　) and a terrible (　　　　).
6. 歯が痛い。 I have a (　　　　).
7. 疲れてへとへとだ。 I'm completely (　　　　) out.
8. 下痢をしている。 I have (　　　　).
9. 便秘がひどい。 I'm terribly (　　　　).
10. 腰が痛くてあまり歩けない。 My (　　　　) hurts and I can't walk well.
11. 脚から血が出ている。 My leg is (　　　　).
12. 足首を捻挫した。 I (　　　　) my ankle.
13. 脚がつった。 I got a (　　　　) in my leg.
14. 階段を上って息が切れた。 I'm out of (　　　　) after climbing stairs.

back	bleeding	breath	chills	cholera	constipated	cough
cramp	diarrhea	dizzy	fever	flu	headache	runny
sprained	stomach	toothache	worn			

Watch the News

First Viewing

ニュースを見て、内容と合っているものはT、違っているものはFを選びましょう。

1. The first hospital which appears in the video has more than ten medical interpreters. [T / F]

2. Most medical facilities in Osaka have interpreters on hand now. [T / F]

3. Some hospitals use remote interpreting systems for medical services. [T / F]

Understand the News　　Second Viewing

1 ニュースをもう一度見て、各問の空所に入る適切な選択肢をａ～ｃから選びましょう。

1. Through the remote interpreting system ____.

a. medical interpreters are immediately dispatched in person

b. automatic translation became available using AI

c. some doctors' tablets are connected to an interpreting center

2. For the Osaka G20 Summit ____ in hospitals.

a. interpreters for five languages were hired

b. tablet devices via the Internet were set up

c. hundreds of volunteers were asked to work

3. According to nationwide medical statistics ____.

a. more than half of the medical institutions have interpreters

b. fewer than ten percent of medical institutions use remote services

c. nearly five percent of hospitals are planning to hire bilingual doctors

2 右の文字列を並べ替えて単語を作り、各文の空所に入れて意味がとおるようにしましょう。語頭の文字群が与えてあるものもあります。

1. If you get injured badly, you will probably need medical (**at**). [netinot]

2. Doctors may have to speak English to communicate with ( ) patients. [oringef]

3. I got a suntan at the ( ) in Hawaii during the summer vacation. [abche]

4. I ate spicy food last night and now my ( ) hurts. [hascmto]

3 CD の音声を聞いて、次ページ News Story の❶～❼の文中にある空所に適切な単語を書き入れましょう。音声は２回繰り返されます。　CD 27

● News Story

Anchor: Japan is expecting an **influx** of sports fans as it prepares to host the Rugby World Cup later this month. ❶ For visitors who find themselves in need of medical attention, the ([1]) ([2]) ([3]) ([4]) ([5]) ([6]). ❷ NHK World's Mayu Ogawa looks at some of the ways hospitals ([1]) ([2]) ([3]) ([4]) ([5]) ([6]) foreign patients.

❶ 言語の壁は問題になり得る

❷ ～との意思疎通の改善を図っている

Narrator: This hospital in Osaka has a department **dedicated to** treating foreign residents and visitors. Today a Brazilian woman has come in for a consultation.

Patient 1: (*In Portuguese*) I cut my foot on a rock at the beach. Is there something I can take?

Narrator: ❸ A medical **interpreter** translates the question from Portuguese and ([1]) ([2]) ([3]) ([4]) ([5]) ([6]).

❸ 医師に状況を説明する

Patient 1: ❹ I can say everything I want to say and I can understand everything ([1]) ([2]) ([3]) ([4]) ([5]) ([6]). It really gives me **peace of mind**.

❹ 医師が私に答えてくれる

Narrator: The hospital has 13 interpreters who speak four languages *between**[1] them, including English and Chinese.

Fujie Teruya (Medical interpreter): I *asked**[2] doctors about certain **technical words** they use or the details of a medical condition. ❺ Then I explain it to patients in ([1]) ([2]) ([3]) ([4]) ([5]) ([6]) ([7]).

❺ 彼らが簡単に理解できる基本的な言葉

Narrator: The hospital is one of only four in Osaka that have medical interpreters **on hand**. Other medical facilities are taking a different **tack**, like this one, which uses a remote interpreting system.

Doctor ***(Tsuneji Shintani):*** What's the issue today?

Patient 2: (*In Chinese*) My stomach really hurts. I didn't sleep at all last night.

Narrator: The tablet is connected via the Internet to a private interpreter center. For the Osaka G20 Summit held last June, **city authorities** installed tablets in 23 hospitals and clinics, offering services in five languages.

❻ Now that the trial period is over, the institutions are considering (　　　　 [1]) (　　　　 [2]) (　　　　 [3]) (　　　　 [4]) (　　　　 [5]) (　　　　 [6]).

❻ そのシステムが彼らの需要に合うかどうか

Shintani: This kind of interpreting service really helps us to provide an accurate **diagnosis** and choose an appropriate treatment.

Narrator: Less than five percent of medical institutions nationwide have interpreters **on site**, and less than nine percent use remote services. ❼ And with Japan (　　　　 [1]) (　　　　 [2]) (　　　　 [3]) (　　　　 [4]) (　　　　 [5]) (　　　　 [6]), to the Rugby World Cup, the Olympics, and the **World Expo**, the influx of foreigners is only going to grow. Mayu Ogawa, NHK World, Osaka.

❼ 近い将来、主催者になる

Notes

＊[1] 文法的には among を使う

＊[2] 現在形 ask だと時制に一貫性が出る

Review the Key Expressions

各問、選択肢から適切な単語を選び、英文を完成させましょう。なお、余分な単語が 1 語ずつあります。

1. 経済的危機の影響でかなり多くの人が職を失い、金銭的な援助が必要となっている。

Because of the economic (　　　　　　), a (　　　　　　) number of people have (　　　　　　) their jobs and are (　　　　　　) (　　　　　　) of (　　　　　　) help.

lost　need　crisis　considerable　necessary　financial　in

2. ただ自分を安心させる［心の平安の］ため、友だちが日本の「ステイホーム」の期間に無事かどうか把握する必要がある。

Just (　　　　　　) my own (　　　　　　) of (　　　　　　), I (　　　　　　) to check that my friends are (　　　　　　) right (　　　　　　) the “stay at home” period in Japan.

piece　mind　for　all　peace　during　need

3. ウォルマートでは、処方箋を調剤するために薬剤師が 1 日 24 時間常駐して［手近に］いる。

At Walmart there is a (　　　　　　) on (　　　　　　) 24 hours (　　　　　　) (　　　　　　) to (　　　　　　) your (　　　　　　).

day　fill　pharmacist　prescriptions　physicist　hand　a

4. 達哉は自分のベンチャー企業でかなり収入を得ているのだから、もう一本立ちしたということだ。

(　　　　　　) (　　　　　　) Tatsuya is (　　　　　　) (　　　　　　) money at his venture (　　　　　　), he is (　　　　　　) (　　　　　　) man.

good　that　own　his　now　firm　making　able

● Discussion Questions

1. What is most difficult for you when you study foreign languages?

2. To stay healthy, what are you more careful about: food or exercise? Why?

UNIT 14

A New View of Hokusai

知られざる北斎の魅力

『新・北斎展 HOKUSAI UPDATED』という題で、有名な「永田コレクション」が公開された。葛飾北斎の活動全期にわたる画業の変遷を紹介する試みである。この展覧会を全体で6章に分ける構成は永田生慈氏が長い間考えてきた企画だったようだ。長期間行方が分からなかった『弘法大師修法図』は北斎の肉筆画の中では最大級のもので、圧巻の迫力を誇る。

● Words & Phrases

CD 28

- ☐ to **flock**　集まる
  People *flocked* to the local farmer's market.
  地域の農作物直売所にぞくぞくと人が集まった。
- ☐ **timeless and borderless**　時空を超えて
- ☐ **impressionist**　印象派
- ☐ **fraction**　ほんの一部、断片
- ☐ **foremost**　先頭に立つ、主要な
  She is the *foremost* violinist of our time.
  彼女は当代随一のバイオリニストです。
- ☐ **culmination**　最高点に達すること、完成
- ☐ to **leave off**　《口語》〈読書などを〉途中でやめる
- ☐ **curator**　学芸員
- ☐ **linear perspective**　直線透視画法
- ☐ **personifying**　具現化する
- ☐ to **strive**　努力する、励む

Before You Watch

以下は、絵画に関する語彙です。下の枠内から適切な単語を選び、空所に入れましょう。なお、余分な単語もあります。

1.	浮世絵	Japanese ( ) prints
2.	宗教画	( ) painting
3.	歴史画	( ) painting
4.	山水画	( ) painting
5.	抽象画	( ) painting
6.	静物画	( ) painting
7.	肖像画	( )
8.	風刺画	( )
9.	油彩画	( ) painting
10.	水彩画	( ) painting
11.	水墨画	Indian ( ) painting
12.	銅版画	( ) print
13.	石版画	( )
14.	落書き	( )

abstract	caricature	copper	exhibition	graffiti	historical
impressionism	ink	landscape	lithograph	oil	pastel
portrait	religious	still-life	watercolor	woodblock	

Watch the News

First Viewing

ニュースを見て、内容と合っているものはT、違っているものはFを選びましょう。

1. Hokusai's *The Great Wave off Kanagawa* influenced traditional artists. [T / F]

2. Nagata spent his own money to buy Hokusai's art works. [T / F]

3. Nagata passed away before the opening of this exhibition. [T / F]

Understand the News — Second Viewing

1 ニュースをもう一度見て、各問の空所に入る適切な選択肢を a ～ c から選びましょう。

1. According to the curator, Hokusai's debut work ____.
  a. is full of originality
  b. imitated his master's techniques
  c. was sold as soon as it was finished

2. The linear perspective technique Hokusai used ____ in Japan.
  a. was not seen very often at that time
  b. has not been very popular since then
  c. was too ordinary to attract people's attention

3. In this large hand-painted work of Hokusai, ____.
  a. the demon represents the evil of money
  b. a Buddhist priest tries to remove the demon
  c. Kobo Daishi saves the demon from disease

2 ニュースに関して、空所に入る適切な数字を下の枠内から選びましょう。なお、余分な選択肢もあります。

1. Hokusai's career as a painter lasted ( ) years.
2. Hokusai's art was influential abroad in the ( )th century.
3. Nagata collected some ( ) pieces of Hokusai's art.
4. Hokusai made a debut as an artist at the age of ( ).
5. Nagata discovered a long-lost work of Hokusai in ( ).

18	19	20	22	70	90	1983	1985	2000	2018

3 CD の音声を聞いて、次ページ News Story の❶～❼の文中にある空所に適切な単語を書き入れましょう。音声は 2 回繰り返されます。 CD 29

● News Story

Anchor: ❶ People in Japan are getting a new perspective on ([1]) ([2]) ([3]) ([4]) ([5]) ([6]). They're **flocking** to an exhibition of work by *Katsushika Hokusai**[1] and learning more about the man and his 70-year career.

❶ 国の、最も偉大な芸術家の一人

❷ ([1]) ([2]) ([3]) ([4]) ([5]) ([6]) a lifelong Hokusai scholar. NHK World's Cathy Cat has more.

❷ その展示は～によって可能になった

Reporter: The appeal of Katsushika Hokusai's art is **timeless and borderless**. People all over the world know his print titled *The Great Wave off Kanagawa*. Sketches by Hokusai was a major influence on **impressionist** painters in the 19th century. ❸ But these works are just a tiny **fraction** ([1]) ([2]) ([3]) ([4]) ([5]) ([6]). Seiji Nagata was the world's **foremost** Hokusai scholar. He used his own money to collect about 2,000 pieces by the artist that had been widely scattered.

❸ 彼の驚くべき、刺激的な遺産の(一部)

Seiji Nagata (Art historian): ❹ We ([1]) ([2]) ([3]) ([4]) ([5]) ([6]) to absorb and learn from Hokusai.

❹ 人々が～するチャンスを作りたい

Reporter: He saw the show as the **culmination** of his research on Hokusai, but Nagata died in February 2018 before the exhibition opened. At this exhibition, 480 pieces that the artist Hokusai created from his debut at 20 to his death at 90 years old are being displayed. The main focus is the Nagata collection. Mika Negishi is picking up where Nagata **left off**. These are some of Hokusai's first works.

Mika Negishi (Curator): This is a work from when Hokusai debuted at age 20. He copied his mentor's work, so there's no originality.

Reporter: But Nagata's collection shows how Hokusai developed his own style. This piece uses **linear perspective**. The technique was rarely used in Japan at that time. Hokusai also took on the challenge of creating this nine-meter-long masterpiece.

Negishi: Looking at the Nagata collection, you see that Hokusai experimented, trying to use new ideas in his own way. ❺ I think we are only now beginning to recognize ([1]) ([2]) ([3]) ([4]) ([5]) ([6]).

❺ 彼が吸収したいろいろな方法

Reporter: Hokusai was ahead of his time in many ways. Look at this print showing a public bath. Hokusai designed it to be cut out and assembled with a light shining behind it to use as a lamp.

I'm really surprised that he already tried 3D in those times because there are so many people, and there's so much detail. It looks so alive! You look inside, and it looks almost as if the people are moving.... In 1983 Nagata made a major discovery. It was big news. Nagata found a long-lost major work by Hokusai in a temple storeroom.

This is amazing! Is this really by Hokusai?

❻ Hokusai ([1]) ([2]) ([3]) hand-painting ([4]) ([5]) ([6]) in his later years. This one shows a demon, **personifying** disease, threatening a Buddhist priest, Kobo Daishi, who tries to *exercise*[*2] the evil spirit. ❼ The exhibition shows that Hokusai ([1]) ([2]) ([3]) ([4]) ([5]) ([6]) and never stopped **striving** to achieve perfection. Cathy Cat, NHK World.

❻ より大きな～の作品に時間をつぎ込んだ

❼（北斎）は自分の作品に決して満足していなかった

Notes

*[1] 葛飾北斎（1760-1849）は、江戸時代後期の浮世絵師。代表作は『富嶽三十六景』や『北斎漫画』など。構成的に力強く動きのある筆法が特徴的で、人物画や風景版画に独自の画風を築き上げた

*[2] excise「除去する」のことと解釈できる

Review the Key Expressions

各問、選択肢から適切な単語を選び、英文を完成させましょう。なお、余分な単語が１語ずつあります。

1. 先生は先週やめたページから英語の授業を始めた。

The teacher started her English lesson ( ) the page ( ) she ( ) ( ) ( ) the week ( ).

off had before has where left from

2. その新しいバレーボールチームはとてもうまいので、まるで、もう何年も一緒にやってきたような感じだ。

The new volleyball team plays ( ) well ( ) it seems ( ) ( ) they have ( ) ( ) together for years.

playing that if so played as been

3. 彼は大学でさらなる高等教育を受けずに、日本版のチェスである将棋に没頭した。

He ( ) ( ) to ( ) *shogi* or Japanese chess, ( ) than ( ) a ( ) education at college.

rather fully devoted playing himself higher getting

4. その靴の質と値段に満足なら、一足買うべきです。

( ) you ( ) ( ) with the ( ) and the price of the shoes, you ( ) buy ( ) ( ).

quality pair are satisfying should a satisfied if

● Discussion Questions

1. Have you ever collected anything: postage stamps, anime figures? If yes, how many and why? If no, why not?

2. What exhibitions or concerts are you most interested in?

UNIT 15 Lighting Up the Nightlife

夜のエンタメ
—— 歴史ツアー

東京の夜のエンターテインメントとして、タイムトラベルというアイデアを利用した歴史ツアーを紹介する。大正末期、昭和初期から 21 世紀の現代へのトラベルは多くの人の興味をひく設定となっている。映像や写真、英語での紹介を交え、外国からの観光客のみではなく日本人にも、古今２つの文化を比べる面白い嗜好になっている。

● Words & Phrases

CD 30

- □ to **cash in on**　～で金儲けする
- □ **in collaboration with**　～と共同で
  He published a book *in collaboration with* his son.
  彼は息子と共著で出版した。
- □ **immersive**　どっぷり浸かった、～浸けの
- □ **ritzy**　《口語》豪華な、高級な〈しばしば皮肉的に使う〉
- □ to **kick off**　《口語》始まる
  The party *kicked off* with the host's welcoming address.
  パーティーは主催者の歓迎の挨拶で始まった。
- □ **footage**　〈映画の〉一場面
- □ **fusion**　融合
- □ to **fall in love**　恋に落ちる
- □ **off limits**　立ち入り禁止区域の
- □ **destination**　目的地

Before You Watch

以下は、旅行や買い物に関する表現です。1～9の空所に当てはまる英語を下のアルファベット表から見つけ、線で囲みましょう。囲み方は縦、横、斜めのいずれも可能です。

例：チェックインしたいのですが。I'd like to (check) in.

- このバスは都心に行きますか。Does this bus go ([1])?
- バス停はどこですか。Where is the bus ([2])?
- この住所にはどう行けばいいですか。How can I get to this ([3])?
- 〈店で〉何かお探しですか。May I help you?
  いいえ、ただ見ているだけです。No, thanks. I'm just ([4]).
- これを試着してみていいですか。Can I ([5]) this on?
- これより小さい（サイズの）ものはありますか。
  Do you have this in a ([6]) size?
- これをホテルまで配達お願いできますか。Could you ([7]) this to my hotel?
- このクレジットカードは使えますか。Can I use this ([8]) card to pay?
- 部屋のエアコンが点きません。The air conditioner in my room doesn't ([9]).

	1	2	3	4	5	6	7	8	9	10	11	12	13	14	15	16
a	C	J	K	G	L	Y	R	W	O	L	Q	S	S	L	C	X
b	H	R	S	O	O	N	U	N	D	O	W	N	T	O	W	N
c	E	R	E	S	E	R	V	A	T	I	O	N	O	O	W	O
d	C	X	A	D	D	R	E	S	S	T	R	L	U	K	P	C
e	K	D	E	L	I	V	E	R	S	T	K	S	T	I	C	K
f	C	A	L	L	H	T	L	I	T	E	R	A	O	N	O	P
g	H	O	S	M	A	L	L	E	R	N	E	Y	O	G	P	T

Watch the News

First Viewing

ニュースを見て、内容と合っているものはT、違っているものはFを選びましょう。

1. Tourists have spent more money per person during the last three years. [T / F]
2. The theme of the tour is early 20th century Japan. [T / F]
3. The picture of Kabukiza was taken in 1923, when the Great Kanto Earthquake occurred. [T / F]

Understand the News　　Second Viewing

1 ニュースをもう一度見て、各問の空所に入る適切な選択肢を a ～ c から選びましょう。

1. The tour guide asks to ____.

a. learn about the famous Japanese jam-filled pastry

b. go to old Japan with the “modern boy”

c. stay longer to see what 2019 looks like

2. The historic clock tower in Ginza ____.

a. is the tallest building in this area

b. belongs to Kimuraya where *anpan* originated

c. is not usually open to any travelers

3. After the show the audience ____.

a. received tickets for drinks served at local bars

b. got various coupons that can be used for their next trip to Ginza

c. was given lottery tickets that may win them prizes

2 以下の各情報を、ニュースに出てきた順序に並べましょう。

1. Tourists enjoy eating *anpan* at Kimuraya.

2. Tourists take pictures at a Ginza’s landmark, the clock tower.

3. “Modern boy” looks surprised because Kabukiza looks so different.

4. The tour guide is now in old Ginza as she hoped.

3 CD の音声を聞いて、次ページ News Story の❶～❼の文中にある空所に適切な単語を書き入れましょう。音声は 2 回繰り返されます。　CD 31

● News Story

***Reporter* (Marie Yanaka):** After-dark entertainment options: It's something the tourism industry is trying to **cash in on**, and this nonverbal art show is no exception. Despite record overall tourist spending, the figures per person have dropped for three years in a row. ❶ So the industry is trying to ([1]) ([2]) ([3]) ([4]) ([5]) ([6]), hoping that they'll spend more too. This group's last performance starts at nine p.m.

❶ 訪問客にもっと長く外出していてもらう

The Japanese government is promoting just that. ❷ **In collaboration with** tourism officials, one of the country's top theater companies ([1]) ([2]) ([3]) ([4]) ([5]) ([6]) ([7]). The firm used its experience putting on shows to create an **immersive** English tour of Ginza.

❷ 先月新しいアイデアを試みた

The walk through the **ritzy** district's historic spots **kicked off** at an established film theater with **footage** set in early 20th century Japan. ❸ It ([1]) ([2]) ([3]) ([4]) ([5]) ([6]), known as the "modern boy" and "modern girl." Suddenly, the actors appeared on stage with a suggestion.

❸ その時代の2人を主役にした

"Modern girl": Let's go out and see [*what*]*1 2019 Ginza looks like.

Reporter: The time travelers, surprised by the changes in the district, gave the audience an interactive way to learn about the city's past. Their first stop: the city's Kabuki theater.

***Tour guide* (Sylvia):** Yes. Yeah. This is Kabukiza. (*Showing picture*) This was Kabukiza in 1923. ❹ Now, you might already know this, but ([1]) ([2]) ([3]) ([4]) ([5]) ([6]) the Great Kanto Earthquake.

❹ これはまた、～があった時だった

Reporter: Then they popped into a 150-year-old bakery to try its famous *anpan*, a Japanese original. The blend of Western bread and the country's bean jam is symbolic of the **fusion** of cultures at the time.

The unique thing about this store is that the participants become fully immersed in the story. ❺ ([1]) ([2]) ([3]) ([4]) ([5]) ([6]), you become part of the reason that the "modern girl" loves present day Ginza. And if you go upstairs, you are right there as the "modern boy" and tour guide **fall in love**.

❺ 一階［階下］にいると決めたなら

Tour guide: Oh, please take me back with you.

Reporter: The tour *guide**2 kept up the act from beginning to end.

The last stop was one of the top symbols of Ginza, a historic clock tower. ❻ It's usually **off limits** but ([1]) ([2]) ([3]) ([4]) ([5]) ([6]) ([7]).

❻ このツアーの参加者は例外［当てはまらない］

Here the story reached a dramatic finish.

"Modern girl": Oh, my God! It's Sylvia!

Reporter: After the show, the audience got tickets for drinks at local bars for more night time fun and spending.

Erina Tokunaga (Nighttime Entertainment PR, Shochiku): There's a trend that people are, people prefer to spend more on experiencing things rather than buying things today.

Reporter: ❼ This theatrical tour is just ([1]) ([2]) ([3]) ([4]) ([5]) ([6]) to enjoy night life that are popping up all over. The hope is that more after-dark entertainment options will encourage visitors to spend more and make Japan the **destination** of choice for international travelers. Marie Yanaka, NHK World.

❼ 多くの新しい方法の1つ

Notes ＊1 ここに what が必要　＊2 語尾に複数形 [z] の発音が聞こえるが不要

Review the Key Expressions

各問、選択肢から適切な単語を選び、英文を完成させましょう。なお、余分な単語が１語ずつあります。

1. 小さな電気扇風機のついた作業服が夏によく売れる。製造者はそれで収益を上げて［儲けて］いる。

( ) clothes with small ( ) fans ( ) very well in the summer. ( ) are ( ) ( ) on them.

manufacturers work in spending electric cashing sell

2. その力士は 15 日間連勝して［連続で勝利し］優勝した。

The sumo ( ) ( ) matches 15 days ( ) ( ) ( ) to ( ) the championship.

in earn wrestler a won front row

3. グレッグは去年のパーティーで、ステイシーを一目で好きになった「～に恋をした」。

Gregg ( ) ( ) ( ) with Stacy ( ) ( ) ( ) at a party last year.

first in fell at love over sight

4. この機会を利用して、皆さんのご協力に感謝したいと思います。

I'd like to ( ) ( ) of this ( ) to ( ) you all ( ) your ( ).

opportunity secure for take advantage cooperation thank

● Discussion Questions

1. If you could travel back in history, which period and where would you like to go? Why?

2. Among the movies you've seen, which was the most memorable? Explain why.

このテキストのメインページ
www.kinsei-do.co.jp/plusmedia/411

次のページの QR コードを読み取ると
直接ページにジャンプできます

オンライン映像配信サービス「plus⁺Media」について

本テキストの映像は plus⁺Media ページ（www.kinsei-do.co.jp/plusmedia）から、ストリーミング再生でご利用いただけます。手順は以下に従ってください。

ログイン

●ご利用には、ログインが必要です。
サイトのログインページ（www.kinsei-do.co.jp/plusmedia/login）へ行き、plus⁺Media パスワード（次のページのシールをはがしたあとに印字されている数字とアルファベット）を入力します。

●パスワードは各テキストにつき１つです。
有効期限は、はじめてログインした時点から１年間になります。

ログインページ

[利用方法]

次のページにある QR コード、もしくは plus⁺Media トップページ（www.kinsei-do.co.jp/plusmedia）から該当するテキストを選んで、そのテキストのメインページにジャンプしてください。

「Video」「Audio」をタッチすると、それぞれのメニューページにジャンプしますので、そこから該当する項目を選べば、ストリーミングが開始されます。

[推奨環境]

iOS (iPhone, iPad)	OS: iOS 6 ～ 13 ブラウザ：標準ブラウザ	Android	OS: Android 4.x ～ 10.0 ブラウザ：標準ブラウザ、Chrome
PC	OS: Windows 7/8/8.1/10, MacOS X　ブラウザ: Internet Explorer 10/11, Microsoft Edge, Firefox 48以降, Chrome 53以降, Safari		

※最新の推奨環境についてはウェブサイトをご確認ください。
※上記の推奨環境を満たしている場合でも、機種によってはご利用いただけない場合もあります。また、推奨環境は技術動向等により変更される場合があります。予めご了承ください。

◀ここからはがして下さい

このシールをはがすと
plus+Media 利用のための
パスワードが
記載されています。
一度はがすと元に戻すことは
できませんので ご注意下さい。

4114 NHK
NEWSLINE 4

本書には音声 CD（別売）があります

NHK NEWSLINE 4

映像で学ぶ NHK 英語ニュースが伝える日本 4

2021年 1 月20日　初版第 1 刷発行
2023年 9 月10日　初版第 4 刷発行

編著者　山 﨑 達 朗
Stella M. Yamazaki

発行者　福 岡 正 人

発行所　株式会社　金 星 堂
（〒101-0051）東京都千代田区神田神保町 3-21
Tel. (03) 3263-3828（営業部）
(03) 3263-3997（編集部）
Fax (03) 3263-0716
http://www.kinsei-do.co.jp

編集担当　西田　碧　　Printed in Japan
印刷所・製本所／大日本印刷株式会社

ISBN978-4-7647-4114-0 C1082

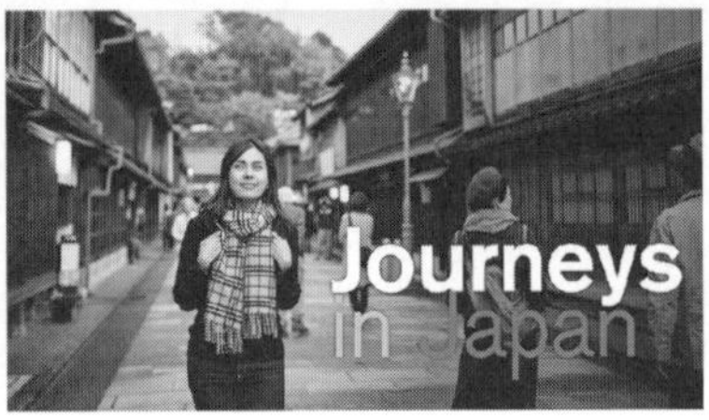